"Moses Wong's journey with God will encourage many who may be going through life's storms.

The God of All Grace has walked alongside him as he journeyed with his daughter Ariel in her medical condition. With a diseased liver and time running out, God had made a way for Ariel and provided a new liver and a fresh lease of life from an unexpected donor.

This book will give hope and comfort to those who are confronted with seemingly unsurmountable challenges. Moses and Charissa have lived through the reality of 2 Corinthians 1:5: 'For just as the sufferings of Christ flow over into our lives, so also through Christ our comfort overflows.'

Indeed God had comforted Moses and Charissa 'in all their troubles and they are able to comfort those in any trouble with the comfort they had received from God' (2 Cor 1:4).

May the God of all comfort encourage you as you read *From Trial to Triumph*!"

~ William Lee
Senior Pastor, *Bartley Christian Church, Singapore*

"*From Trial to Triumph* is not just another book; it is an inspiring testimony of how a journey along life's arduous road was pursued to victory!

Along the way, things seemed to go wrong in an unending nightmare. It took the courageous spirit of Bro. Moses to revisit those painful moments and share his story so that others can be encouraged to see the bright side of life and have a living hope to press on should they face a similar difficulty.

I am very heartened to see the elements of faith, perseverance, humility and love in Bro. Moses, when he tried to cling on to the Captain of his life in an effort to bring his family through their storms.

From Trial to Triumph is a true story that is spiritually stirring, bringing hope to readers who are weathering their own storms in life. May they be encouraged by Bro. Moses' testimony, and put their faith in the Lord Jesus, the Captain of our lives!

Sola Gracia!"

~ Rev. Anthony Loh
Senior Pastor, *Jurong Christian Church*

"This is one of the most intense books that I've read in my life!

I praise God and commend Moses for his tremendous effort to share with us his family's pilgrimage in the Lord so humbly and honestly. This book has impacted me with a renewed sense of the greatness of God's mercies, lovingkindness and faithfulness with a deep encouragement and appreciation of my friend's perseverance and faithfulness in trusting and walking in the Lord through life's most difficult challenges.

In Moses' recounting of his family's journey of their life's unexpected problems, pressures and pains, I am reminded of the sovereignty of God's work leading us to know Him more deeply through our trials. I marvel at the abounding grace of God that is available to us his children to sustain us in all circumstances. I am amazed at how the faithfulness and tangibility of God's love shines through in so many ways to strengthen and carry his children through this fallen and broken world. And I am encouraged to keep trusting and obeying my Lord Jesus Christ in my life through Moses' life and story.

I highly recommend this book to everyone!

To God be the glory."

~ Hon Chin Foang
Lead Pastor, *Good News Baptist church*

———◆———

"*From Trial to Triumph* tells the touching story of a loving father as he struggles with his baby daughter's desperate prolonged health crisis. We were moved as we read this honest heartfelt account of God's incredible faithfulness during a time of great trial and the invaluable lessons and insights the Lord gave to Moses Wong. In Appendix B, Moses shares five priceless principles for overcoming trials that will help parents with the challenges they face. We highly recommend this book to all parents."

~ Dr. Rick & Laurel Langston
Missionary Teachers, *Campus Crusade of Christ International for 48 years*
Founding Faculty, *International Graduate School of Leadership Philippines and East Asia School of Theology in Singapore*

"Praise the Lord as another 'star' shines in the dark. Moses Wong, the author witnessed the gracious hand of the Lord in leading, moulding and training him during a tough situation to be a blessing and hope for others. This book opens up to us Moses' struggles and growth during a very trying time in his life, when his beloved daughter, Ariel, faced a life-threatening medical condition.

Do you have a sick child to nurse? Do you fear losing your loved one? Have you faced the emotional turmoil of many setbacks and waited long hours for a miracle to happen? This book will offer a glimpse of the possible answers and the hope we have in our struggles and pains. A great and almighty God is always present as our 'invisible guest' to help us in times of need.

Moses demonstrates the importance of having strong family support in times of trouble. A supportive spouse like Charissa is a gracious gift from God to him to weather the hardships and trying moments in his life. As a loving and united family, they will continue to witness and write their stories about our great and gracious God.

As their pastor before, I can testify that our God is good and gracious to prepare, provide and protect His children to grow in maturity towards Christ-likeness. Do read and share this inspiring life testimony with your loved ones.

Immanuel!"

~ Rev. James Ng
Senior Minister, *Glory Presbyterian Church*

———◆———

"In this book, you'll find the reality of miracles and the practicality of the Christian faith. You will also find sound advice in times of trials, especially for husband and wife. Fathers will certainly get cues on how to be a firm leader of the family and what to do when trials come into your territory. This is a good book — easy to read and with some suspense that would keep you flipping page after page."

~ Rev. Reynaldo G. Navarro
Filipino Ministry Pastor, *International Baptist Church*

"In his book, *From Trial to Triumph*, Moses bares his heart in caring for his medically-challenging daughter, Ariel. He chronicles for us the faith-stretching moments and the steps he took as he was confronted with challenging situations. What comes across very clearly from his poignant reflections is he has remained steadfast and unwavering in his faith in God in trying times. In the end, Ariel is healed and God is glorified!"

~ Rev. Lam Kok Hiang
Country Director, *Cru Singapore*

———◆———

"Thank God for the lives of Moses Wong and Charissa's family. They went through a challenging and faith-testing time with their daughter, Ariel, and the Lord healed her. Indeed this is a miracle! Praise be to God! Their lives' story will be a great encouragement and inspiration to others."

~ Tay Choon Mong
Board Member, *Cru Singapore*

———◆———

"Moses has poured his heart and soul into this life-changing book. It takes a man of utmost strength to write a book on such a personal journey. I believe Moses has written this book to inspire other parents to walk in faith. Kudos to you and your awesome family, Moses!"

~ Gideon F.
Mukwai, *Story Coach*

MOSES WONG

FROM TRIAL TO TRIUMPH

A personal account of a father's heart
in caring for his medically-challenged child

From Trial To Triumph

Copyright © 2016 by Moses Wong
All photos are by Moses Wong

Published by Journey With U Pte Ltd
UEN. 201223582M
Copyright © 2016
151 Chin Sweee Rd, #01-43/45
Manhattan House
Singapore 169876
Tel: +65 9843 9404
http://journeywithu.com
Email: moses@journeywithu.com

ISBN-13: 978-981-09-8703-9

All Scripture quotations, unless otherwise indicated, are taken from the Holy Bible,
New International Version®, NIV®. Copyright ©1973, 1978, 1984, 2011 by Biblica, Inc.™
Used by permission of Zondervan. All rights reserved worldwide. www.zondervan.com
The "NIV" and "New International Version" are trademarks registered in the
United States Patent and Trademark Office by Biblica, Inc.™

All rights reserved.

No part of this publication may be reproduced or transmitted in any form or
by any means electronic or mechanical, including photocopy, recording,
or any information storage and retrieval system now known or to be invented,
without prior written permission of the author. Requests to the author
should be addressed to moses@journeywithu.com

12 16   01

SPECIAL BONUS
FROM MOSES WONG

Now that you have your copy of *"From Trial to Triumph"*, you are on your way to creating effective strategies for coping with your child that has medical challenges. Plus, you will be inspired with the hope and love to continue your journey with your kids.

You'll also receive the special bonus I have created to add to your toolkit—"Five Helpful Principles in Overcoming Trials", which is a list of pointers that helped me to move from trial to triumph. These will serve as great reminders to help you sustain your faith and hope on this journey. Post this page in a place where you can review it daily.

There's so much confusing information out there about how to stay grounded in your faith when you are faced with significant challenges with your kids. When you finish this book, you'll be armed with what you need to know to not only cope with the situation but to strengthen your faith and trust in God's grace and unending love.

While "Five Helpful Principles in Overcoming Trials" is offered for sale, as a special gift from me, you can claim it for free here: http://FromTrialtoTriumphBook.com/gift

The sooner you discover and apply effective ways to cope with the medical situation of your child, the sooner you can help your family and grow spiritually from what may appear to be a very dire situation.

May the messages in this book help you find hope, inspiration, and love to continue the journey with grace and gratitude.

Moses

CONTENTS

Chapter 1

TO TRUST OR NOT TO TRUST? THAT IS THE QUESTION!

We had been actively trying for our third child for two years but to no avail. At that time, my wife and I already had two older children: Chloe, who was six years old, and Ezekiel, who was three. We thought that a three-year gap between each child would be ideal. A three-year-old would be quite independent when the baby came. However, this was just human planning and wisdom. God had other plans that we weren't aware of.

By 2006, we genuinely believed that our "baby-making factory" had closed shop. Then a miracle happened! My wife, Charissa, suddenly found herself pregnant. It was a pleasant surprise for us because we had already given up hope of having a third child. We were so excited to be Daddy and Mummy again for the third time.

Things were pretty smooth sailing until Charissa went for her fifth-month pregnancy scans. Our gynaecologist revealed shocking news to us: the baby was suspected of having Down syndrome. The only way to confirm that was to go for an amniotic fluid test, which was quite expensive. We did not choose this option because as Christians, we would never consider aborting the foetus even if the baby was confirmed to have Down syndrome. The amniotic fluid test would only make sense only for those who might abort the foetus if the baby had Down syndrome. To us, a foetus is a life and therefore we would never terminate a life. The joy of having a third child immediately turned into a period of trial, testing our faith in God.

It saddened my heart whenever I saw Charissa in tears. As the head of our family, I could only encourage my family to believe in God—a God who knows best. Every day we would pray, read God's Word, and ask Him for His deliverance. According to our gynaecologist, the only way to know if the baby had Down syndrome was when she was born.

I would never forget one evening when my wife was so heartbroken. She was in tears as we sat on our white, linen bed.

She broke down sobbing, "Why has such a thing happened to us? I thought God is a loving God. How could He give us such a gift? Isn't it true that a loving Father will give the best gift for His children? What should we do now? We can't abort the foetus. It is a life and it will dishonour God if we do it."

I was speechless as I was listening silently to her grievances. I did not know how to respond to her in a loving way that was comforting and encouraging. So I thought the best way was to keep quiet, listen and say nothing.

Occasionally, I would hug my wife, and let her lean on my chest as she continued sharing her thoughts. It was easy for me to say positive words or give the 'model answers' to her questions, but it was Charissa who was going to carry the baby to full term, not me.

My two older children were busy with their routines. Chloe was playing her piano, while Ezekiel was watching his favourite television programme. It was a long and woeful night.

In my prayer, I asked God, "Lord, how could this child be a blessing? I don't understand You."

He said, "You have read that children are blessings from Me, am I right? Do you believe in what you have read in the Bible?"

I said, "But, aren't You supposed to be better than my earthly father? Even my earthly father would not give me a snake if I asked for a fish. Surely You are much better than my earthly father?"

He said, "I have a higher purpose for you than you know. Though you may not understand it now, can you trust in My heart for you and your family?"

I said, "Lord Jesus, I don't know where You are leading us. But I choose to trust in Your daily guidance and wisdom."

He said, "This is where you need to have faith in Me."

I was literally shaking when I finished my prayer. I had to share with my wife what God had instructed me. Before talking to her, I was not sure if she would accept my words or not. But I knew that this was the only thing we could do.

Finally after nine months of pregnancy, the moment came when Charissa was wheeled into the labour ward. We were so anxious. We did not know what God's plan was for us. We had prayed to God, and we had trusted Him all the way. When the gynaecologist told us that our baby girl was a normal baby, we were overjoyed. We named our baby Ariel. God had delivered her from Down syndrome!

In fact, in our hearts, we had decided that Ariel would serve God full-time if He delivered her. When celebrating her first month (as all Chinese families do), we dedicated her to serve God as His servant. We had indeed tasted the goodness of God!

We may not understand why God allows certain trials. But as long as we don't give up trusting Him, He will direct our paths accordingly. It is our duty to save and protect life as He desires.

If we honour God, God will honour us.

Learning Points

1. God's plan and timing is always better than ours.

2. Believe in God and His Word rather than our circumstances.

3. Sometimes, a quiet listening ear and gentle hug is all you need to give someone who is suffering.

Reflection Questions

1. What are some recent events that have happened in your life where you have tried to take control of?

2. What does God and His Word say in relation to these events?

3. Do you find it hard to believe that God is in control of these events? Why?

Suggested Prayer

"Lord Jesus, I thank You for these events (name them specifically) that have happened in my life. Though I may not understand the reasons behind them, I choose to believe in You and Your Word rather than the circumstances. Help me with my unbelief and grant me the faith to trust You to see me through. Amen."

Chapter 2

What Can You Tell From a Baby's Poo?

I never thought that the colour of a baby's poo—which all of us take for granted—would be something I yearned for. Have you ever yearned for your baby's poo?

I know it is a weird question. For me, however, it was special.

You see, just when my wife and I thought that the crisis was over for Ariel, we were not prepared for another major setback. Initially, Ariel was born with a mild jaundice, which was common for most babies. In fact her paediatrician told us there was no need to have any more follow-up sessions. So we didn't really suspect anything was wrong about Ariel's physical condition.

However as the days progressed, her skin turned more and more yellowish. Our friends from church alerted us that there was something amiss about Ariel. By that time, Ariel was about seventy days old, and she should be less yellowish if her liver was maturing. In fact, prior to discovering Ariel's liver problem, we consulted a medical doctor about her condition and the same assurance was given to us that there was nothing to be concerned about. However we decided to seek a second opinion just to confirm the diagnosis. Never did we realise that there was a 'tsunami' awaiting us.

The second paediatrician told us that Ariel was suffering from a rare form of liver malfunction, which happened to one in 10,000 babies. We were dumbfounded. Our faith in God was once again shakened. "How could this happen to Ariel again? I thought You had just delivered her from Down syndrome."

We were told that Ariel was born with an absence of bile ducts. The medical name for this condition is Biliary Atresia. The only permanent cure was to have a liver transplant. As Ariel was just a baby, she was too tiny to have a liver transplant. So a temporary measure was to do a Kasai operation using the small intestine to act as a bile duct. The main purpose was for her to increase her weight to about 10 kilograms so that she would be big enough to have a liver transplant. We were utterly devastated by the treatment plan. There were so many questions in our minds. "Would she survive this Kasai operation? Who would donate a liver for her transplant?"

I am not sure if you have ever been confronted with such a situation. What thoughts would flash through your mind if you knew that this could be the last time you would see your precious little baby whom you nurtured through the past nine months of pregnancy?

Floods of emotions overwhelmed us at that moment. We were fearful that we might lose Ariel during the Kasai operation. We were also confused by God's plan for Ariel. On the one hand, she had experienced God's deliverance from her suspected Down syndrome, but now she was experiencing another major crisis that might cost her her life.

In addition, we also felt hopeless about such a treatment. It was an operation that would prepare her for another major operation—the liver transplant. We were trapped between the devil and the deep blue sea. There was so much emotional turmoil in us that we didn't have the privilege of time to process everything.

We were not given much time to consider. We needed to make an immediate decision. To increase the chances of having a successful Kasai operation, she needed to be operated on as soon as possible. So within five days upon discovery of this depressing news, Ariel ended up on the operation table.

I still remember vividly that as I was carrying Ariel in the hospital ward the night before the surgery, I was in great agony. "Would I see Ariel again? Would this be my last time carrying my little baby?" It was a difficult and long night for me. I experienced pain that was beyond description.

While waiting for the surgery to be over, I went into a breastfeeding room to pray. I needed God's presence and assurance at that moment. That day was 30 March 2006. So I turned to the book of Proverbs, chapter thirty, verse thirty, in the Bible, which says that the lion is mighty among all beasts and retreats before nothing. Why Proverbs? Because Proverbs is a book of wisdom in the Old Testament, and I needed God's wisdom in Ariel's situation. I was ministered by my God because Ariel also means "Lion of God". To me, it meant that Ariel, this lion of God, would overcome all obstacles. She would overcome this surgery. I was grateful for God's encouragement.

One important sign to know if the Kasai operation was successful was the colour of Ariel's stools. If the stools were greenish or dark, it meant that the Kasai surgery was a success. So each time Ariel passed motion, we would be very nervous. Before we opened up her diapers, we would pray fervently that we would see coloured stools. But it didn't happen. The stools were whitish. We were very discouraged and disappointed by the results. I really did not know what would happen to Ariel. My heart was broken, and I decided to pray and fast for Ariel's recovery. When I did that, a miracle happened the next day. Her stools turned greenish. When I saw that, I cried with tears. I said, "Thank You, thank You Jesus."

Even though the colour of Ariel's stools started to improve, I did not stop my prayer with fasting. I was determined to see complete healing in Ariel. At that point, the colour of her stools was inconsistent. Sometimes, they were whitish. Sometimes, coloured. Another reason why I did not stop my fast was because her jaundice level had not dropped since the Kasai operation. Theoretically, if the bile started to flow out through her small intestine, the jaundice level should have dropped. However that had not happened yet.

During that period of fasting, God was very merciful to us. A friend who was also a pastor from another church came down to pray for her by anointing her head with oil. It was a very significant ceremony for Christians as it represents God's presence and blessings upon Ariel. A patient's mummy, whom we just got to know, strangely had a burden for Ariel and asked her church's pastor to pray for Ariel. We were grateful to experience God's tangible love for us.

Finally on my thirty-seventh day of prayer and fasting, Ariel's jaundice level began to drop for the first time from 151 to 113. We were so thrilled! I took it as a sign that God had indeed heard my prayer and I broke my fast finally. By that time, I had lost about nine kilograms. I closed my fast with another verse in the Bible. It was taken from my daily reading from the book of Psalms. In Psalms 147:11, it says, "The Lord is pleased with those who worship Him and trust His love." Amen.

So our baby's poo colour has a special meaning to us. It is a sign of life, no longer an irritation, as most of us may think. It is yet another reminder that Ariel, God's lion, is still the king of the jungle.

Learning Points

1. Though human beings may make mistakes, God never does.

2. Keep on trusting God even when you are confused by His plan for you.

3. When God is all you have, He is all you need.

Reflection Questions

1. Describe an incident where you are confused by God's plan for you.

2. Are you able to keep on believing His best for you? Why?

3. How do you demonstrate that God is all you need?

Suggested Prayer

"Lord Jesus, I confess to You that I fail to understand Your purpose for me in this incident (name the incident). Help me to keep trusting You even though I am confused. Thank You that You are all I need in whatever situation I may be in. Amen."

Chapter 3

Number 41

At the end of 2006, we had to sell our HDB flat and move into my mother-in-law's house. Living with in-laws is a challenge, but it was a move that brought with it many unprecedented blessings.

When we first discovered that Ariel had a liver problem, our eldest daughter, Chloe was already in Primary One. I recall that particular day when Ariel was admitted to KK Women's and Children's Hospital (KKH) for a detailed scanning to confirm the diagnosis. I had to rush down to pick up Chloe from her school at about 6.30 PM. Since there was no one at home (as Charissa was in the hospital ward with Ariel), I would have to bring Chloe to KKH.

Once I brought Chloe to the hospital, she would bathe and do her school work there. By the time we reached home, it would be about midnight. The next day, after sending Chloe to school at 12 PM, I would go back to KKH to accompany

Charissa and Ariel. I repeated this routine for the next few days. It was incredibly tiring for us.

We figured that we needed an extra pair of hands to take care of our two older children while we devoted ourselves fully to caring for Ariel. It was not fair for our older two children to "suffer" together with us—even though I was sure that they wouldn't mind.

Thus, at the end of 2006, we decided to sell our HDB flat and moved in with my mother-in-law.

Packing our things for the shift and caring for Ariel at the same time was a nightmare. However, we knew that we had to move to get extra help for our two older children. We are grateful that my mother-in-law and our friends helped us throughout the shifting process. God provided the transport and the movers at a very affordable price. Thankfully, Ariel's condition was stable and there was no sudden medical emergency during then that required our immediate attention.

In the new school that Chloe would be going to, she would be in Primary Two. This posed to be a difficult situation for us. Schools normally would not have vacancies for Primary Two students, unless their parents had to work overseas and their children had to transfer out.

To complicate matters, the school we desired Chloe to attend was a reputable primary school, Pei Hwa Presbyterian Primary School (Pei Hwa, for short). We would like her to be there, not because the school was reputable, but rather because it was near my parents-in-law's home and Chloe's cousins were also studying there. Therefore it would be more convenient for our parents-in-law to bring their grandchildren to Pei Hwa all at one go. Chloe would also have some familiar faces in her new school, and we hoped that this would make the transition a little easier for her.

The first thing that we did was to write to the Ministry Of Education (MOE) to request for a change of school for Chloe due to Ariel's medical condition. We thought that it would not be an issue. But we were wrong! We were surprised to receive a letter from MOE that they couldn't accede to our request because there were no vacancies at the schools near my in-laws' home. "How could that be?" we asked ourselves. "You mean that the school can't even squeeze in one more student on compassionate grounds?" We thought it was a ridiculous answer.

So the next thing we did was to approach our Member of Parliament (MP) for help. The MP was kind enough to write a letter on our behalf to MOE. This reply was slightly better. Chloe was assigned to Bukit Timah Primary School, an alternative school near my in-laws' home. However, we were not fully satisfied.

We decided to see Reverend James Ng, senior pastor of the church supporting Pei Hwa Presbyterian Primary School. He also happened to be the pastor who went through the marriage preparation course with us before our wedding. When we were there, Reverend James told us that it was not the church's policy to interfere with the school's administration. He told us that even his church's elders were not guaranteed a place for their children in Pei Hwa. However, he suggested, "Maybe you could go to Pei Hwa now to see Mrs Foo, their newly appointed principal. We just finished our meeting with her in the morning before you came. I believe she is still in the school. See if she can help you."

We were a little surprised when we heard that. Immediately we said goodbye to Reverend James and zoomed down to Pei Hwa. We went to the school's general office to request to speak with Mrs Foo. The school's administrative clerk asked us, "May I know what is it regarding?"

"Oh, we want to transfer our daughter, Chloe to this school. We hope that Mrs Foo is able to help us," we replied.

"I am sorry to say that it is usually quite tough for a new Primary Two student to join the school unless some students are transferred out due to their parents' overseas posting," the clerk responded.

"We understand that. That's why we are here to see Mrs Foo. We'd like to explain our situation to her and hopefully she can help us. We know that Mrs Foo is in the school. Are we correct?" we pressed on.

"Yes she is, but she may be too busy to see you. Why don't you write in?" the clerk replied.

We knew that this was not the best way. The school received so many letters and the clerk might just discard our letter.

"No, we really need to speak to Mrs Foo to explain our situation. We can wait for her until she is free to see us." We were adamant.

We waited outside the office, standing firm in our request to see Mrs Foo because we knew that she was in the office, as informed by Reverend James Ng earlier in the day.

As it turned out, just when we'd almost lost all hope, a lady walked to the reception area. Somehow, Charissa had a hunch that she was the principal, and she dashed into the office.

"Are you Mrs Foo?"

"Yes," she replied.

"We really need to speak to you about our request to transfer our daughter to this school. Can we have five minutes of your time?" we asked politely.

"Sorry I am busy now. I am not sure when I will be free to see you," Mrs Foo responded.

"No problem, we are willing to wait till you are free. But you must see us as you promised," we reminded her gently.

We were able to converse with Mrs Foo eventually. We could sense that she was sympathetic towards our plight. However, she did not promise us anything. She told us that there was the MOE's teacher-pupil ration that she had to abide by. However, she ended the session by saying, "Pray to God and trust Him for the results."

We left the session feeling that we had done our utmost in trying to get Chloe into Pei Hwa. We knew that God had to do the rest.

When we did not hear from Pei Hwa when the school term started, we were disappointed. We asked God, "Why didn't You answer our prayers?" We were heart-broken.

When we called up Pei Hwa, we were told that the school needed one more week to reply to us officially. We were advised to let Chloe temporarily attend Bukit Timah Primary School, as assigned by MOE.

Towards the end of the first week, the phone rang one evening. We were so tired. We really did not want to take it. We had had a long and bruising day. Just before it rang for the last time, my wife picked up the phone and the caller said, "Congratulations! Your daughter has been granted special admission into Pei Hwa Presbyterian Primary School."

We were stunned, and literally shaking with joy. We could not believe it was true!

After Chloe's first day in Pei Hwa, we asked her, "How many students are there in your class Chloe?"

"Forty-one," she replied.

"Forty-one?" we responded in shock.

"Yes, forty-one!" she repeated.

We were amazed because MOE's guideline for school's teacher-student ratio is a maximum of forty students to one teacher for each class.

Our daughter, Chloe was #41. God was in control.

Learning Points

1. After we have done our best, God will do the rest.

2. The so-called "coincidences" are God's divine guidance in our lives. Nothing happens by coincidence.

3. God's work always amazes us.

Reflection Questions

1. Take a moment to pause and reflect. Have there been any coincidences that happened to you recently?

2. What do you think is God's purpose for you in this coincidence?

3. Are you surprised by such a coincidence?

Suggested Prayer

"Lord Jesus, I know that nothing happens by coincidence. The people that I met, the event that happened, they are all part of Your divine guidance for me. Help me to be willing to co-operate with Your work in my life that I may be continuously amazed by You and give You the glory You desire. Amen."

Chapter 4

TRUST GOD IN MY WORK

Because of Ariel's frequent admissions to hospital, it became very disruptive to my work. Ariel was prone to having infections and fever spikes, something we had no control over. She could be normal and healthy in the morning, and in the afternoon, she could suddenly become weak and feverish. We were told by the doctor-in-charge that whenever she had a fever spike, we had to send her to the Accident & Emergency Department. Very often she would be given two weeks' antibiotic treatment before her normal temperature returned.

I could sense that my team leader was not too happy about it even though she did not verbalise it. Maybe it was because we were working in a Christian organisation and we were supposed to be gracious towards one another. I could fully understand her predicament. "Who would want a worker in her team that suddenly disappeared from his work?" I wouldn't want to have such a team member either.

So finally during one of Ariel's admissions, while I was at the hospital ward with Ariel, I received a text message from my team leader, "Moses, we understand that you are facing difficult challenges in your family. In view of your situation, it will be better for you to be transferred from your present role to the Human Resource department. From today onwards, you no longer need to report to me. The Human Resource manager will get in touch with you soon and advise you accordingly. God bless." In short, I was transferred from my present job!

I was shocked to receive a text like that while I was still in the hospital with Ariel.

Though I was hurt by it, I reckoned that it might be God's will for me to take care of my daughter and serve Him at the same time.

Frankly speaking, I felt guilty for not contributing to my work, especially when my company was gracious enough to continue giving me my salary in spite of my frequent absenteeism from work. I had seriously thought of resigning from my job, so that I could focus on taking care of Ariel. I wanted to quit mainly because I knew that my daughter, Ariel needed me to be with her at the moment. There were many people who could cover my job in the organisation, but how many fathers did Ariel have? If I wouldn't sacrifice my time for her, who would? Who would bother about her?

Secondly, I wanted to quit so that I would not make things difficult for the HR manager who wanted accountability of my time since the company was paying me. It was not an easy decision to make. I did wonder that if I quit, who would provide for my family? Honestly I didn't know. I told myself, "I could only trust God one step at a time."

When I asked God about it, I knew that He wanted me to stay. How did I know? We knew because we received many prayers and financial help from friends who stood by us during this trying period.

One incident that I cannot forget was when a medical student came to interview us as an intern. Through the conversation, I found out she was a believer. Somehow, we were able to converse well with one another. I was vulnerable enough to share about God's work in my life and the challenges that I was facing. The next day, I received an envelope from her. I opened up the envelope and saw a cheque of ten thousand dollars!

I was pleasantly surprised. She told me that she had shared about my situation with her father and God prompted him to give. What an amazing grace of God! How could I not stay on in the job He had called me to? Eventually, I decided to stay on to show my gratitude towards God and my friends who believed in us.

One "crazy" thing that I did during this period of time was to take up a twelve-month diploma course in Human Resources (Training and Development). Why did I do that?

The main reason was that when I was assigned to the HR department, I was tasked to take charge of staff development. But I had no prior HR experience and qualification! So to do my job well, I decided to equip myself through formal studies. I believed that this was the best way of spending my time in the hospital besides taking care of Ariel. I couldn't go anywhere, but surely I could read my course materials and do my assignments in the hospital!

There were times when I needed to skip certain lessons due to Ariel's medical condition, and my wife couldn't take over as she too was busy with her work. Thankfully I had supportive coursemates who would fill in the gaps for those lessons I missed out. In the end, I graduated unexpectedly with a Silver Award. All glory to my God who guided me one step at a time!

I recall an incident when I needed to travel overseas for a work-related conference in Bangkok. It was a tough situation to decide whether to go or not to go. I was struggling with these thoughts: "If I choose not to go, I wouldn't be effective in my work. If I choose to go, what if Ariel's condition suddenly turns bad and needs an urgent admission? I won't be there for her." Finally, I decided to go for the conference, prepared to come back any time if my family needed me.

It was difficult to concentrate at the conference. It was a global HR conference where all the top HR practitioners came together to discuss strategies and experiences that empowered the company to greater heights. Whenever my mind was preoccupied with a lot of "what ifs", I would pray and tell God that I would trust Him to take care of Ariel. He was ultimately in charge of everything. All I asked was that wherever I was, I would be fully present because He was in control. It was such an attitude and faith in my God that carried me through my work's challenges with calmness and confidence.

Without God, I could not survive or even thrive in my work. In fact, after two years in the HR department, I was promoted to Assistant HR Manager. All glory be to my God!

LEARNING POINTS

1. Parental responsibility cannot be delegated.

2. Trust God one step at a time.

3. Wherever you are, be all there.

REFLECTION QUESTIONS

1. What are some work challenges you face as a parent?

2. How do you plan to resolve them?

3. Are you able to fully focus on the task God has called you to do in spite of your challenges?

SUGGESTED PRAYER

"Lord Jesus, I ask of You to grant me wisdom to manage my challenges at work as well as caring for my family's needs. Let me trust You one step at a time, and where You place me, I will be fully present and aware that You are in ultimate control of my situation. Amen."

Chapter 5

A Time of Busts and A Time of Booms

Throughout our journey, we were hit with ups and downs, challenges and victories. It was indeed a time of busts (lows) and a time of booms (highs). In a matter of days, we went from sweat, tears, fears to cheering the Lord. I am sure if you were in my shoes, you would have felt the same. You wouldn't understand our mixed emotions, until you understand what my family was going through.

One of the main purposes for Ariel to go through Kasai surgery when she was about seventy days old was to buy time for her to put on weight so that she would be big enough to go for a liver transplant before she turned three years old.

To ensure that Ariel could achieve this, the doctor recommended her to consume a specially-formulated milk powder called Generaid Plus which was imported from the United Kingdom. One tin of five hundred grams of Generaid

Plus would cost us seventy dollars, and Ariel could finish it in about three days. This milk powder alone would set us back by at least seven hundred dollars a month. We were burdened by such an expensive milk powder. In spite of the huge expenses, as parents wanted to give our best to our children.

Upon receiving our first delivery of Generaid Plus, I accidentally noticed something interesting on the invoice; there was a Bible verse written on it. A thought came to my mind: "Maybe I could ask for a special discount for bulk purchase?" I wasn't sure if it would be approved. Anyway there was no harm trying. So I emailed the director, explaining our situation and asking for his special favour upon us. The director replied that it was not the company's policy to give special discounts to customers. However he could initiate a special arrangement for the money to be passed back to us. We were blown away by the director's special grace to us— Ariel received his life-saving milk powder for free!

We also had an interesting encounter with a Nursing lecturer who recommended us an alternative therapy upon listening to our woes about Ariel. The alternative therapy was called "Jin Shin Jyutsu". We were interested to explore this form of therapy because it did not require any form of oral medication. Basically it is using your fingers to press at certain acu-pressure points for a few minutes to harmonise meridian flows in your body.

The doctor-in-charge did not object to such treatment as there was no medical evidence to suggest whether it worked for or against the patients. It belonged to the category of "no harm trying". By some divine arrangement, we got connected with Siew Kim, the founder of Jin Shin Jyutsu in Singapore. It was not easy to arrange to meet her as she had a full schedule of appointments each day. Somehow, because of our persistent request, she agreed to squeeze out fifteen minutes from her lunch time to see us. We were so delighted by her kind gesture.

After treating Ariel for the first time, Siew Kim told us that she felt for Ariel, and would like to continue seeing her. She usually treats her patients for forty five minutes each session, and that would cost one hundred dollars. However since Ariel was still a baby, she could only treat her for fifteen minutes each session, and she would do it for FREE. We were so surprised and touched by her generosity. We could only respond in gratitude to God that He indeed cared for Ariel's needs.

As Ariel progressed towards a liver transplant, we were also concerned about the gigantic medical expenses. Just the operation alone would incur thirty thousand dollars cash, even after government subsidies. We didn't know how we could afford it. Somehow we believed that God would see us through.

I can still recall a very interesting encounter with a medical student by the name of Joanne (mentioned earlier in Chapter 4, but I shall elaborate more here). I was wearing a T-shirt that bore the words "Gen12", which was a short-term missions project organised by my company. As Joanne was involved in Gen12, we got connected. As Joanne got to know us more, she became very burdened for Ariel. She took the initiative to share about Ariel's needs with her parents. The next day, she came back with a cheque of ten thousand dollars for Ariel's medical expenses. She told us that it was her parents' love gift for Ariel. We were astounded by it. We never expected this extraordinary providence of God.

Besides these, my company's director, Mr Lam Kok Hiang called for donations among the staff to be given to Ariel's medical fund. My church pastor, Rev. Lim Pang Jong also raised some funds for us. Interestingly, another church that I worked very closely with for community outreaches also initiated a church offering for Ariel's medical costs. On top of that, many individuals also gave generously too.

We were just so overwhelmed by God's tangible expression of His provision through churches and friends around us. Even before the scheduling of her liver transplant, the funds needed to cover the expenses had already come in. All praises to God's name!

As I look back, all I can say again is that it was a time of busts and a time of booms.

LEARNING POINTS

1. God's grace is evident in every challenge we face.

2. God's provision is always beyond our expectations.

3. God watches over every step of our trials.

REFLECTION QUESTIONS

1. What are some challenges you are facing?

2. Are you able to identify God's grace in them?

3. Are you aware of God's provision and guidance throughout the entire process?

SUGGESTED PRAYER

"Lord Jesus, I thank You for the challenges in my life. I acknowledge that they are God's given opportunities for me to trust You for Your grace, guidance and provision. Strengthen my faith in You. Empower me by Your Holy Spirit as I go through them for Your glory. Amen."

Chapter 6

FACING DEATH EYEBALL TO EYEBALL

Initially we were not open to consider being living donors for Ariel's liver problem. Being staunch Christians, we were determined to trust God for only ONE way to cure Ariel, and that was God's divine and miraculous healing in her without any human intervention.

We brought her for many miracle services organised by different charismatic churches. We even brought her down to Suntec City to see an anointed prophet from Africa to ask him to pray for healing for Ariel. We had also tried Holy Communion, a Christian ritual to ask for God's healing for Ariel. Whatever you can name, we probably would have tried it. But all these were in vain.

We had also attempted to give Ariel different kinds of health supplements such as *ling zhi*, bee pollen powder, cactus juice, etc. They were suggested to us by friends out of goodwill that hopefully these could help Ariel solve her liver problem.

I remember an incident when we gave Ariel a triple dosage of *ling zhi* because the sales person claimed that it had helped a patient with a similar problem. In our eagerness to heal Ariel, we tried that on her. The effect was disastrous. She passed out so much soft and liquid stools that she became seriously dehydrated. As a result, she had to be admitted to hospital for observation. When Professor Quak Seng Hock, the doctor-in-charge of Ariel asked us what happened to Ariel, we dared not tell him that we had given her too much *ling zhi* for fear of being reprimanded by him. All these efforts were again in vain, in spite of spending a few thousand dollars on these supplements.

The wake-up call came in August 2007 when Prof. Quak told us that we needed to seriously consider finding a living donor for Ariel's liver transplant. By that time, Ariel was already one year and eight months old. It was either a "now or never" decision. It was "now" because Ariel was well enough to receive a new organ. It was "never" because if we delayed the decision for the transplant for too long, Ariel might become too sick and weak to receive a new organ.

We were faced with a tough decision upon hearing this news. Our faith in God was momentarily shakened. "Shall we trust God for His divine healing all the way till Ariel's last breath or should we schedule a liver transplant for her?" As we prayed about it, we felt that it would be too unbearable for us to see Ariel gradually dying before our eyes, when as parents, we could do something for her.

With that, we decided to schedule her for a liver transplant. Charissa was the natural and only choice as she shared the same blood type as Ariel. Though we had decided to go for it, it was a tough journey preparing for it.

First, Charissa had high cholesterol levels. She had to lower it to a healthy level before a transplant was a possibility. Otherwise, she might suffer a heart attack during the transplant operation. She could lower it either by taking medication (which of course had side-effects) or by natural means through a strict diet and regular exercise. So what happened next was that Charissa kept eating fresh onions and garlic as well as jogging regularly with me. We did it for one month, and when Charissa went for her blood test, the result did not show any improvement. We were disheartened but we did not give up. Finally, three months later, Charissa's cholesterol level dropped to a healthy level.

Second, Charissa was a dormant hepatitis carrier. We never knew such terminology existed until she went for a thorough medical test on all her organs' functions. The implication would be that the liver transplant might possibly trigger this dormant hepatitis to be active again. We didn't know how that could happen but we were told to be prepared that should it happen, Charissa could be an active hepatitis carrier who might suffer from liver failure eventually.

These two factors, namely, her high cholesterol level and being a dormant hepatitis carrier showed that Charissa was not an ideal donor, but we had no other options.

We would never ask our siblings to consider being a living donor because it was a major operation. There was always a small possibility of donors dying during a transplant, and they had dependents to take care of as well.

Third, we suffered a trauma related to surgery. My father-in-law went for a heart bypass operation a few years ago, in 2002. As he was certified fit for this surgery, nobody would expect that he would not pull through the operation. According to the surgeon, there was only a one percent fatality rate, and it happened to my father-in-law!

The surgeon had done more than one hundred and fifty heart bypass operations and this was the first time that a patient died during the operation. He couldn't explain what had gone wrong. In short, nothing was definite in a surgery no matter how small the percentage of fatality might be. In fact, prior to Ariel's liver transplant, we read from the newspaper that a living kidney donor had died during a kidney's transplant.

Our most important concern was Charissa's health. We were told to let nature take its course, meaning to wait for a dead donor to come, rather than risking Charissa's life. We knew that if we did that, it was like sentencing Ariel to death because most liver patients died while waiting for dead donors.

My dad was one of them. He had been a liver patient for ten years. There were three occasions when he was admitted to hospital for a possibility of a liver transplant. But each time it turned out to be a disappointment, because when the surgeons cut open the cadaveric donors, they found that their livers were not suitable. My dad eventually died of liver failure, because he forbade any of his sons to donate part of their livers to him. He knew that the risk was too high for them, and they had their own families to take care of.

We understood people's concerns for us. We knew fully well that we couldn't afford to have another patient in the family should anything go wrong for Charissa during the transplant. We had two young children—Chloe who was then eight years old and Ezekiel, five years old. To be honest, I was not prepared for the worst-case scenario: to take care of two patients (Charissa and Ariel) plus two young children. I would have gone crazy and be devastated if that happened to us.

It was a dilemma for us. We could only pray for God's mercy to be upon us and for His courage to move on. What needed to be done for Ariel had to be done. A liver transplant was the only medical intervention that could possibly save Ariel. As parents, we would never give up on our children. We could only deal with one thing at a time.

Learning Points

1. Don't have a preconceived idea of how God would heal.

2. Medical intervention, though done by humans, may be considered as God's way of healing too.

3. Manage your crisis one step at a time.

Reflection Questions

1. Do you have a preconceived idea of how God should heal?

2. Are you open to God's alternative way of healing?

3. Do you limit God to heal in certain ways only?

Suggested Prayer

"Lord Jesus, forgive me for limiting Your way of healing. Your ways and thoughts are definitely higher and better than mine. Grant me wisdom to make a right decision in order to complete Your healing in my life. Amen."

Chapter 7

PREGNANT WITH DESPAIR

It was only in November 2007 when the blood test finally showed that Charissa had successfully lowered her cholesterol level to the acceptable level that qualifies her to go for a liver transplant. However, something happened to Charissa in December 2007 that made it impossible for her to be a living donor. She was pregnant!

We couldn't believe it initially. In fact, Charissa's first month of pregnancy was quite unstable. There was minor bleeding and we thought it could either be a false pregnancy or miscarriage. However, in the second month of her pregnancy, things stabilised and Charissa was confirmed pregnant.

We were in a dilemma. "How should we explain to churches and friends who have given to Ariel's liver transplant operation costs, now that Charissa is not eligible to be a living donor? How could we be so careless to allow such a thing to interfere with the operation?" We started to ask God about His intention for us and for Ariel.

As we prayed, we knew that it was God's supernatural intervention. It was His way of telling us that Charissa shouldn't go ahead to be a living donor because we were not prepared for the worst-case scenario. It was difficult to break the news to people around us about Charissa's pregnancy. When people asked us, "What is going to happen to Ariel?" Our response was, "We don't know. You need to ask God. He is the one who stopped the transplant from happening to Ariel."

This pregnancy was depressing for us as we were constantly concerned about Ariel's condition. Nothing pains the parents so much as to see their children dying gradually before them and they couldn't do anything to help. In our case, we could actually help Ariel by having my wife be a living donor, but our plan was disrupted by this sudden pregnancy.

"Lord why do you allow such a thing to happen to us? By right, we should be happy with Your blessings. But now, we can't because we will be losing Ariel. We are so tempted to abort the foetus, but we know that we can't. Because if we do that, we will be killing a new life. But how else can we save our precious daughter, Ariel? She is so cute and adorable. We can't bear to lose her. We are so lost and helpless now. Only You can save her now. Grant us the courage and faith to move on. Please hear our cries and help us to move on, Jesus."

It pained my heart to see my wife, Charissa wash her face with tears almost every day. Every day, she would sob and ask me, "Why does God allow this to happen? We are going to lose Ariel!" I was irritated whenever I heard her asking me the same question again and again. I tried to be empathetic in my listening to her. However there were moments I wanted to scream at her and say, "Please stop! We need to be strong for our children!" I was glad that I did not do that. I just felt so stressed to face a situation with no apparent solution.

"Lord, please do something now before I lose my sanity and patience. I don't know how long I can be a support to my wife before I burst out and get burnt out."

According to the doctor-in-charge, Charissa could only be a living donor again six months after she has given birth. By that time, Ariel might not live long enough to receive it. We were sad to hear that, but we had to rely on God's strength and courage to move on.

We also heard some negative and useless comments like "Why were you so careless?" We chose to discard them and believe in what the Bible says that every child, including our fourth one, is a blessing from God. When Charissa finally reached her fifth month of pregnancy, we were hoping that this fourth child would be a boy. Why? So that it would not be a replacement for Ariel. But the scan's result turned out otherwise. It was a girl. Our faith in God started to waver. "Are You giving Shiloh (our fourth daughter) to us because You are going to take Ariel away? Please help us to trust in Your will, Jesus."

This depressing nine-month pregnancy finally ended when Shiloh was born in July 2008. When we held this new baby in our hands and heard her cry, we knew that in our hearts Charissa could not be a donor anymore. Shiloh would need the presence of a mother to love and nurture her. The stakes became too high for Charissa to be a living donor. It would be unfair for Shiloh to grow up without a mother's presence should any unexpected thing happen to Charissa during the liver transplant.

By that time Ariel was already two-and-a-half years old. Statistically, babies born with such a rare liver problem would not be able to survive till the age of three without a liver transplant. Time was running out for Ariel. There were only two possible options left for Ariel. "God, You either heal her supernaturally or You provide a dead donor for her transplant. Whatever it is, it will still be considered a miracle for us."

Learning Points

1. Believe in the truth of God's Word in spite of your circumstances and what others may say.

2. Be honest and transparent with God about your emotions and struggles.

3. Be strong for your spouse and your family by the Holy Spirit's empowerment.

Reflection Questions

1. Are you able to confess your emotions honestly to God?

2. Are you able to hold on to the truth of God's Word in spite of your circumstances?

3. Can you be strong for your spouse when she or he is weak in faith?

Suggested Prayer

"Lord Jesus, help me to be a tower of strength for my spouse and family in the midst of trials and challenges. Grant me a mustard seed of faith to believe in You and Your Word in spite of my circumstances. Amen."

Chapter 8

A CLOSE CALL

When Ariel was about twenty-six months old, she started to pass out black stools. This was her first sign of end-stage complications. The black stools implied that there was internal bleeding. The hardening of a person's liver would eventually cause the blood vessels along the food tube to burst, resulting in internal bleeding. We didn't see blood stains in the stools because it was a gradual bleeding that happened a few days ago.

Doctors suggested putting Ariel on a six-hour fast, so that they could do an endoscopy to plaster all the burst blood vessels. All these were just temporary measures to stop the internal bleeding. As the liver hardened, pressure would start to build up again along the food tube and would cause other blood vessels to burst eventually.

To stop Ariel from eating for six hours before the endoscopy was a torture for us. Very often she would cry herself to sleep because she was too hungry. Even after the endoscopy, we couldn't feed her immediately. The whole process would take about five or six days before she could be discharged from hospital.

As the days progressed, Ariel began to pass black stools more frequently. These often happened without much warning. She could be very happy and alive in the morning, and the next moment, become lethargic and lifeless.

Whenever we saw black stools, we knew that we had to send her to the Accident and Emergency department. It could be as often as two admissions per month. In fact, I didn't even bother to unpack my stuff after each discharge from the hospital. The hospital became my second home. I even knew exactly where to get the cheapest food and coffee inside the hospital!

Besides staying in the hospital due to black stools, Ariel was often admitted to drain water out of her tummy. The medical term for such a condition is "ascites". It is an accumulation of fluid in the abdominal cavity. The development of ascites indicates advanced liver disease and Ariel should be referred for consideration of a liver transplant as soon as possible.

There were at least two occasions that Ariel could have passed on. In October 2008, while Ariel was in hospital to treat her end-stage complications, her body suddenly shook violently. It was about 6 AM, and I happened to be sleeping beside her. The next moment, her temperature shot up to 40.8 degrees Celsius. It was a scary scene. I thought I was going to lose her any moment. I quickly called the doctor in the ward to check her body's condition. The doctor told me that the bacteria had gone into her blood stream to attack her organs. Thankfully Ariel was in the hospital then, so they could administer the antibiotic intravenously. This saved her life! What a close shave!

Then subsequently from October to December 2008, there were at least two occasions when Ariel, out of nowhere, vomited fresh blood at home. My wife and my eldest daughter screamed when they saw it. Fortunately I was there when these happened. After Ariel vomited blood, she became dizzy. She was not able to stand or sit anymore. My mother-in-law would then use newspaper to clean the blood on the floor, while we called for an ambulance.

When the medics finally arrived, they checked her blood pressure and gave her oxygen. Once they stabilised her condition, I carried her in my arm and brought her to the ambulance. While we were walking along the common corridor, she threw out more fresh blood. It was a frightening scene.

It was a matter of life and death.

When I was in the ambulance, I was heartbroken and helpless. I asked God, "Is this the time You are going to take Ariel home?" It became very scary when Ariel's blood pressure started dropping and the ambulance sounded its siren on our way to the hospital.

Surprisingly Ariel overcame all these close shaves. I didn't know how she did it. Somehow, she overcame them all by the grace of God. She was truly the lion of God as her name, Ariel implied; a lion that never gave up, a lion that retreated before nothing.

In mid-December 2008, Ariel was admitted for her end-stage complications. She was in Intensive Care Unit (ICU) for internal bleeding. While we were there, something traumatic happened. There was a big commotion outside our room. A group of doctors and nurses were pushing a baby on a hospital bed into an ICU room. They looked very nervous and anxious. I didn't know what happened. I was naturally curious. Then I saw a familiar face. I knew this woman. Her one-year-old baby girl also suffered the some liver problem as Ariel. I went out of my room and had a conversation with her. From there I found out that her baby girl's heartbeat had suddenly stopped due to a bacterial attack. They were in the normal ward when this happened. That was why they were rushing her into ICU.

When I heard this, my heart sank. This could also happen to Ariel. I am sure it was a traumatic blow to the baby's mother. What happened was a scene I would never forget. Our my room was just next to this baby's ICU room, I could see that doctors and nurses were working tirelessly to revive the baby. I could see that many tubes were attached to her body and blood was draining out from the tubes. I couldn't bear to see it anymore. It was such a heart-wrenching and depressing scene.

The doctor told the mum that even if the baby was revived, she would not last for three days as her other vital organs have been damaged. But the mum didn't want to give up on her baby. Who would, anyway? She insisted that the doctors do their best to save her baby.

That night I went home highly disturbed. I prayed for God's miracle for this baby. Before I left the hospital, the doctors were still working very hard to save the baby. The next morning when I came back, the room was empty. The baby was gone.

I was very sad. This was like a precursor to how Ariel could be dying if nothing happened to save her. It would be beyond my threshold if I were to see Ariel dying that way. If I were the baby's mum, I would say, "Stop saving her. Enough is enough! Please let her go. Please don't torture my baby girl anymore."

When Ariel was finally discharged from hospital, I brought the entire family together that same night, and we knelt before God and interceded for Ariel. As we prayed, I wept like never before. I was very sad and depressed, especially after what I had just witnessed. We prayed to God, "Ariel has suffered enough. We can't bear to let her suffer anymore. Either You perform a miracle to heal her completely or You take her away peacefully. Though we will be very sad if You do the latter, but at least we know that she is free from suffering. And we know that we will see her in heaven when we are there eventually."

After the prayer, we were determined to see her die peacefully at home rather than being tortured at the hospital. At least she was going to our Father in Heaven.

Nothing torments parents so much than to see their children dying gradually before their eyes, and yet they can do nothing to alleviate their children's pain.

Learning Points

1. When fears and uncertainties surround you, remember to come to God in prayer.

2. God can use a crisis to strengthen a family.

3. Be prepared to die (because we are going to heaven) and yet be ready to live (because miracles can happen anytime, anywhere).

Reflection Questions

1. How would you normally respond to fears and uncertainties?

2. Do you allow crises to strengthen or weaken your family?

3. Do you sincerely believe that going to heaven is the best thing for us as Christians?

Suggested Prayer

"Lord Jesus, help me to remember that I can always come to You with my fears and uncertainties because You promise that You will never leave us nor forsake us. Let me be always prepared to die yet ready to live for Your glory. Amen."

Chapter 9

GOD'S MIRACLE!

The next day—27 December 2008—one day after Ariel was discharged from hospital, I was attending a friend's daughter's one-month celebration when her mother told me that my wife was looking for me urgently.

Charissa told me that the hospital called her to inform her that there was a possibility of a liver transplant for Ariel. I couldn't believe it! My heart was beating very fast upon hearing the news. She told me that Ariel needed to be admitted to the hospital immediately to prepare for a liver transplant.

"Really? How could God answer our prayer so fast and so unexpectedly?" Without delay, I left my friend's place. I asked my friend, Jessie to remember Ariel in prayer. I was still having trouble believing what I just heard. "Is it true that Ariel is going to receive a new liver? How unbelievable!"

We finally reached the hospital at about 2 PM. Charissa could not join us because she just sprained her ankle. Upon reaching the hospital's ward, I tried to ask for confirmation regarding this liver transplant. The doctors told me that they couldn't be sure either. The only way to confirm if there was an operation was when the surgeon received the organ personally and deemed it fit for Ariel. As of now, we had to prepare, as if Ariel was definitely going for a liver transplant.

So for the next ten hours, they had to put Ariel on a total fast to prepare her for the operation which might or might not happen. "Ariel needs to suffer again. I hope her suffering would not be in vain." This was my prayer to God.

The next moment, I saw the nurses bathe Ariel and put on a surgical suit over her. It was like she was really going for the transplant. As I was sitting with her on the hospital bed, I was praying and singing Christian songs to comfort her and myself. I dared not ask our friends to pray because I was afraid that if the transplant did not take place (like in my Dad's case), I would need to go through the long process of explaining to them. And honestly, I didn't have the strength to manage that. So here I was alone with my beloved daughter, waiting for the moment to come.

It was the longest, toughest and most torturing afternoon for me. "Is Ariel going for the transplant or is she not? Who can tell me the answer please?" Then, a scary thought came to me, "What if the transplant fails? We will not have Ariel anymore. If her body rejects this new liver, it will be 'game over' for her. We will lose her forever." In other words, these could be my last few hours to hold her alive before the transplant begins. By then it was already 6 PM.

When Charissa asked me about the status, I told her that we needed to assume that Ariel would be going for the transplant unless the surgeon called it off. Thus far, there was no news that it was called off. I also told her, "You'd better come to the hospital because it may be your last chance to see her." Thankfully my sister-in-law was free to fetch her and our older children here. As a family we once again prayed and committed Ariel into God's loving hands. I had also decided to pray and fast for Ariel.

I didn't know how I managed to go through all this waiting. It was like waiting for an executioner to appear and lead me to the execution site. Finally at about 12 AM on 28 December 2008, the ward's door opened. Ariel was pushed out of her room, clad in a surgical robe, with the nurses and doctors around her. Regardless of their race or religion, the medical staff told us that they would be praying for Ariel. We were very moved by their kind gestures.

A group of doctors and nurses pushed Ariel towards the operating theatre, while we followed behind, with Charissa on the wheelchair due to her swollen ankle. By this time, I had already texted our friends, requesting for prayer.

I was surprised to receive a phone call from Mr Lam Kok Hiang, my company's director. He said that he and his wife, Sharon would like to drop by to pray for Ariel. So they came—our first physical prayer warriors.

Initially I planned to stay overnight at the hospital. But the nurse told us that the operation would take at least ten to twelve hours. She suggested that we should go home and rest, so that after the surgery, we could have all the strength and energy to take care of Ariel. On her advice, we decided to go home and rest.

That night when I was resting on my bed, I was in tenterhooks. I didn't know when and how I fell asleep. The next day, I was woken up by a phone call from the hospital at about 10 AM. The nurse informed us that the operation was over and Ariel would continue to stay in the surgical ward until her condition stabilised. We cried for joy on hearing that. We thought that Ariel's ordeal was over but little did we know that there was another emotional roller coaster awaiting us.

LEARNING POINTS

1. God's miracle usually happens in those moments we don't expect it to happen.

2. Crises often unites people of different races and religions.

3. The Lord grants peace and rest for those He loves and cares.

REFLECTION QUESTIONS

1. As you go through a crisis in your life, do you still hope for God's miracle?

2. Are you able to experience God's peace and rest in a crisis? If not, what can you do differently to experience it?

SUGGESTED PRAYER

"Lord Jesus, I thank You for the crises in life as it is an opportunity for me to trust You and to experience Your peace and rest. Lead me in Your righteous path and grant me peace beyond human understanding. Amen."

Chapter 10

MIRACLE MYSTERY DONOR

It all happened so fast. At the eleventh hour. Just when we had lost all hope, that was when the miracle happened. A mystery donor had appeared from nowhere!

When I first received the phone call from the hospital about this dead donor, I did not have much information. I understood that under the Transplant Act, the donor's family and the recipient were not allowed to be in contact with one another. The main reason was so that the recipient's family would not feel obligated to offer monetary compensation to the donor's family, should they request for it.

A few months after Ariel's transplant, we read something in the newspaper about the donor's family.

It was a tragic incident of a 16-year-old student who collapsed in school while engaging in a school activity. She was declared brain-dead upon arrival at the hospital. I had no doubt that it was a heartbreaking moment for her parents, to lose a seemingly-healthy girl suddenly to some unknown virus.

At that moment, they were asked to consider donating their girl's organs to save patients who were in need of an organ transplant urgently, and they had only twenty hours to decide!

Upon hearing the news, I was dumbfounded. I finally understand the reason why God needed to delay His answers to our prayer. To have a dead donor for Ariel, someone had to die. In our case, God had chosen to provide a liver for Ariel through a sixteen-year-old girl. Her parents' loss became our gain. If I were God, it would be so tough for me to have to decide to exchange one parent's happiness for another parent's sorrow.

I am sure that it was already a very traumatic and painful experience for them to lose a daughter just like that. Now, to allow doctors to cut their daughter's body to harvest her organs for other patients must be pain beyond imagination.

I'm guessing that logically, they knew they should donate her organs to save lives; but emotionally they must have experienced a searing pain to allow this.

Finally on their monk's advice, they made the logical decision to allow the surgeons to harvest their daughter's organs. They donated her eyes, liver, kidneys and whatever that was still functioning, to save more than seven lives altogether. When I read about it, I was speechless and teary-eyed.

There is no doubt in my mind that it took exceptional courage to turn their tragedy into happiness for others who were desperately in need of an organ. For having such a deep sense of humanity, my family is forever blessed and grateful.

We are grateful because their selfless decision has given Ariel an opportunity to live healthily. On the other hand, we are sad because two parents had lost their precious child.

"What if they had refused to make such a donation? What if they had delayed beyond twenty-four hours?"

We don't have the answers of what could possibly have happened to Ariel and the many others, if they decided not to donate, or delay their donation. We are eternally grateful for what they have done, and the timing of it all was simply miraculous.

As I write this chapter, I am still overcome by the mixed feelings I experienced that day. Somewhere deep in my heart lies a letter that reads:

Dear Mystery Donor, parents and family members,

Thank you so much for your gift of life to Ariel. Without your courageous decision to give your daughter's liver to Ariel, she would not have lived to see this day. Your sacrificial giving has given us hope and light in this arduous journey with Ariel.

It was through Ariel's liver disease that we experienced the wonder of human kindness. It was through Ariel's liver disease that we saw how God parted the Red Sea before our very eyes.

Learning Points

1. Someone's loss may be another person's gain. Trust God for His perfect timing.

2. God has His purpose for delaying His answer to our prayer (though we may not understand His reasons).

Reflection Questions

Is there anyone you would like to appreciate? If so, write a letter of gratitude to him or her now.

Suggested Prayer

"Lord Jesus, I am amazed and speechless by Your miraculous provision. Forgive me for being too selfish about my own needs without considering the needs of others. Help me to believe that Your provision is always timely and perfect. Amen."

Chapter 11

The Potter and the Clay

When we reached the hospital and saw Ariel in the Intensive Care Unit, we were so distraught to see that there were about eight tubes attached to her body—one at the nose, one at the mouth, two at the neck, one at the stomach, etc. We were so pained to see her in such a state, though we were mentally prepared that she would be like that after surgery.

Watching her on that bed, I felt like a knife had pierced through my heart. I asked the surgeon-in-charge, "Will my daughter make it? Will she?"

He replied politely, "We have done all humanly possible."

"So what is next?" I pressed while choking.

"The first fourteen days are critical. They can make or break," he responded. As he was talking, he lifted up his index finger, "The rest is really up to the One above."

We nodded our heads and replied, "We understand. We will trust God for the result."

Ariel was sleeping in an isolated room. Outside the room were some paintings of The Little Mermaid and Winnie the Pooh. There were a few nurses and doctors at the nursing station, busy checking the patients' records using their desktop computers. Everyone looked very serious. No one was seen chatting or smiling. The room was very cold and quiet.

Ariel's condition was closely monitored with many blood tests done at three hours' interval. I wondered how Ariel could ever produce enough blood for all these tests. I can tell you that her blood tests results were like the stock market—with erratic up-and-down fluctuations. Each movement swung my heart like a roller coaster. Sometimes the markers went up, and then the next moment, they would come down suddenly. So our emotions were literally hung upon those minute-by-minute fluctuations. Those were very tense moments for us. Each day was like an eternal suffering for us. The only thing we could do was to pray for God's mercy and healing for Ariel.

I also decided to enter into another period of fasting for Ariel. As her Daddy, this was the least and the best thing I could do for her—interceding before God on her behalf. We were encouraged by the numerous friends and relatives who came to comfort us. Some of them had prayed with us outside the ICU. As I shared about Ariel's situation with them, sometimes I just couldn't control my emotions and my tears would just roll down my cheeks. I was crying like a baby before my friends and relatives.

As I waited upon the Lord, the image of the potter and the clay came to my mind; God was the potter and I was the clay. Before the clay could be a beautiful finished product, it had to go through the furnace of fire for a period of time. But the clay would not be destroyed in the process because God, the Potter was looking intensely at the clay to ensure that it would emerge beautifully as a polished product, reflecting the image of God. I was strengthened and renewed daily during this period of waiting for God to perform another miracle for Ariel.

Besides the unstable blood test results, one of the biggest challenges was that a lot of fluids (about three thousand litres per day) were passing through Ariel's tummy. It was a lot compared to her weight which was about ten kilogrammes. The surgeons couldn't understand such a phenomenon. As I continued to pray for Ariel, on my twelfth day of fasting, I was assured of God's victory over her life as I read the book of Jeremiah, chapter thirty-one, verses eleven to thirteen from the Holy Bible. These verses talk about God's promise to redeem Israel from Babylonian captivity. He will turn their mourning into gladness and the priests will feast on God's abundant provision. To me, the message was clear. He would redeem Ariel from this sickness, and after redemption was jubilation—joy, dancing and feasting. With that confirmation, I decided to break my fast on 12 January 2009.

Two days later, a miracle happened. The fluid from Ariel's tummy was suddenly reduced to only two hundred millimetres. It was like God had turned off a water tap. The doctors were greatly surprised.

They asked me, "Mr. Wong, what did you do?"

"I should be asking you, what did you do?" I replied.

Later, I told them, "I did nothing but prayed." The doctors shook their heads in disbelief. I shook mine in relief. I am sure they concurred with me that God, the Potter had stepped in to cut off the tap so as to dry up the clay.

As the days progressed, things were getting brighter. Ariel's fever, that had been unsettling since the transplant, was gone. Her blood's clotting time had improved from twenty-seven seconds to seventeen seconds (normal is less than fourteen seconds). Her liver function's tests had improved accordingly. Her tummy's size had also shrunk from sixty-eight centimetres to sixty centimetres. During that time, I had lost five kilogrammes, thanks to my fasting.

Finally, after one month of stay in the hospital, Ariel was declared healthy enough to be discharged from the National University Hospital, ward forty-two, bed six on 24 January 2009.

The night before her discharge, I recalled the Lord's goodness and faithfulness in this heart-wrenching, three-year journey with Ariel. I wrote them down and entitled it, "God's Amazing Grace", which you can find in Appendix A. As you read it, may you be encouraged in the Lord in your life's challenges.

As we thought that Ariel's ordeal would soon be over, we were wrong! A few months later, Ariel contracted the H1N1 virus. "OMG! How long must we suffer? Is this going to be an end for Ariel?" These were the questions that came to our mind.

At that point in time, the H1N1 virus was relatively unknown to the World Health Organisation. There was no known cure for such a virus. When Singapore first detected her first case in March 2009, we were very concerned. We were told that such a virus would adversely affect the elderly and children, especially those with underlying medical conditions. And Ariel was a three-year-old child and she has a medical condition!

It first started with my eleven-year-old daughter who was down with a fever spike. After confirming that she had contracted the H1N1 virus, we knew it was too late to prevent it from spreading to Ariel. Subsequently, my mother-in-law, my eight-year-old boy and my wife all contracted the virus, except me. We were praying very hard that Ariel would be protected from it because we knew that she belonged to the high-risk category. When Ariel suddenly had a fever spike after all family members had contracted the virus, we knew that she had gotten it too.

Fear and anxiety immediately set in. We prayed to Jesus desperately, "Jesus, we have suffered enough for the past three years. Why do You allow this to happen again? We don't believe that You delivered Ariel from such a major crisis, and then let her fall by the HIN1 virus. We pray against the virus and we declare Your power and victory over the virus. Please don't disappoint us."

Immediately she was admitted into the isolation ward for observation. We were very upset with God. We questioned God, "Are You going to take her away after performing such a great miracle in her life? God, please don't play with us. We can't take this any longer. Why did You bother to perform miracle after miracle if You wanted to take her away eventually? How would that glorify Your Name? We are perplexed; we are confused; we are disheartened. Please don't fail us again, Jesus."

The next few days were really torturing for me. There was so much uncertainty about this virus and what could possibly happen to Ariel. As usual, we could only pray and plead God for His mercy upon her. There was no medication to treat this virus. It had to run its course. We could only trust God that He would not test us beyond what we could endure. Finally, after one week, Ariel's condition became better and she was able to be discharged from the hospital.

Thank God that this was the final episode in Ariel's life that warranted a crisis intervention.

Ariel, the lion of Judah, has finally overcome!

Today, Ariel is a ten-year-old girl, studying happily in Pei Hwa Presbyterian Primary School. She is a testimony of Jesus' love and faithfulness to our family; and yes, the lion of Judah.

As I recall this most challenging part of my parenting journey, I can only say that these three years were like walking through a long and dark tunnel, with my hand holding Ariel's hand tightly. In every of my steps, I didn't know exactly what to do, or where to go, or who to turn to for advice and what the outcome would be. I only knew that God has entrusted Ariel to me, and it is my responsibility as Ariel's Daddy, to surrender her daily to God and walk continuously by faith. The light at the end of the tunnel is my firm belief that God, who has called me to be a father to Ariel, will be faithful to see us through from Trial to Triumph!

Learning Points

1. Prayer is the best thing, not the least you can do as a Christian.

2. The clay must go through a furnace of fire for a prolonged period before it can emerge as a beautiful finished product.

3. God will not allow trials in our lives where His grace is not sufficient to see us through.

Reflection Questions

1. Is prayer your natural act of response whenever you face trials and challenges?

2. What does the image of a potter and clay tell you about God?

3. Do you believe that God's grace is always sufficient for us in every trial and challenge?

Suggested Prayer

"Lord Jesus, I praise You for helping me to understand the true meaning of a potter and clay. Your lovingkindness is far greater than what my finite mind can ever imagine. Let me be transformed and renewed as I move from trial to triumph, that I may declare Your awesome deeds. For Your glory, Amen."

SPECIAL BONUS
FROM MOSES WONG

Now that you have your copy of *"From Trial to Triumph"*, you are on your way to creating effective strategies for coping with your child that has medical challenges. Plus, you will be inspired with the hope and love to continue your journey with your kids.

You'll also receive the special bonus I have created to add to your toolkit—"Five Helpful Principles in Overcoming Trials", which is a list of pointers that helped me to move from trial to triumph. These will serve as great reminders to help you sustain your faith and hope on this journey. Post this page in a place where you can review it daily.

There's so much confusing information out there about how to stay grounded in your faith when you are faced with significant challenges with your kids. When you finish this book, you'll be armed with what you need to know to not only cope with the situation but to strengthen your faith and trust in God's grace and unending love.

While "Five Helpful Principles in Overcoming Trials" is offered for sale, as a special gift from me, you can claim it for free here: http://FromTrialtoTriumphBook.com/gift

The sooner you discover and apply effective ways to cope with the medical situation of your child, the sooner you can help your family and grow spiritually from what may appear to be a very dire situation.

May the messages in this book help you find hope, inspiration, and love to continue the journey with grace and gratitude.

Moses

GOD'S AMAZING GRACE

It's God's amazing grace that…

…He provides a new liver for Ariel via a liver transplant which was perceived as an impossibility by her doctors as most liver patients die while waiting for a dead donor.

It's God's amazing grace that…

…He provides at His perfect timing, for without it Ariel may not live to celebrate her three-year-old birthday.

It's God's amazing grace that…

…He provides the best liver for Ariel. If not for His supernatural intervention by giving us another baby, Charissa would have donated her liver, which is definitely less ideal than the liver of the sixteen-year-old girl.

It is God's amazing grace that…

…He provides people of different faiths to pray for Ariel while she was going through her transplant operation which lasted for seven-and-a-half hours. We were very touched when nurses and doctors, whether they were Chinese, Indian or Malay told us that they would be praying for Ariel as she was being pushed into the operating theatre.

It's God's amazing grace that…

…We could pull through so many hospital admissions all these years without falling sick at all. It is not an exaggerating to say that we have become "permanent residents" at NUH. We even know where to get the cheapest coffee and food!

It's God's amazing grace that…

…We could pay for all the hospital bills without declaring ourselves bankrupt. We were grateful that more than thirty-five friends and relatives plus churches gave generously for her transplant, which cost more than one hundred thousand dollars before government subsidies.

It's God's amazing grace that…

…Our children did reasonably well in their studies even though we did not have much time to coach them. Chloe, our eldest daughter received a good progress award for her Primary Four results!

It's God's amazing grace that…

…We could still serve the Lord in Cru Singapore and in church with so many constraints and uncertainties. Many times, we were tempted to quit but somehow each time when we prayed about it, the Lord increased our capacity to serve Him.

Right now, we are trusting God that…

…It will be God's amazing grace to complete His healing on Ariel, as she needs six months to one year to stabilise her condition.

…It will be God's amazing grace to continue to provide for Ariel's medical costs, that is, one thousand dollars per month, as she needs to take anti-rejection pills which are expensive drugs and she has to take them for life.

…It will be God's amazing grace that one day Ariel, this lion of God will "roar" for Jesus through her life testimony.

How amazing is God's grace for us!

==

This write-up is a tribute to God by Moses on 25 January 2009, the date prior to Ariel's discharge as he reflects on God's mighty works in Ariel's life through this three-year journey. The night before the unplanned liver transplant, he and his wife cried out to God desperately, "God, You either heal her or take her home." And the rest is history.

Update:

It has been seven years since the life-saving operation. Ariel is growing healthily today and just needs regular check-ups every three months. Also, thanks to the government's scheme of enabling insurance to cover pre-existing conditions, her medical costs per month for the anti-rejection pills has gone down significantly from one thousand dollars a month to just one hundred and fifty dollars per month. We thank and praise God for His goodness and work in Ariel's life!

FIVE HELPFUL PRINCIPLES IN OVERCOMING TRIALS

As I reflect on the useful principles that carried me through that trying period, I would like to use the acronym TRIAL to summarise them. They are not in order of priority.

1. Tell others what you need

It is not easy for some of us to express our needs to other people. We like to be self-reliant and feel embarrassed to trouble others. Most of us can live quite well without help from other people when life goes well.

But when we were faced with a medically-challenging baby, this was NOT the case.

This was a major crisis that required us to mobilise all possible resources to help us manage it well. To make matters worse, it was a long-term crisis that could last as long as our child's lifetime. It was like walking through a dark tunnel without seeing any light at the other end. We needed to cast our human pride aside and say the three MOST important words: I NEED YOU to...

When I was with Ariel in the hospital, sometimes I needed to go out alone to have a breather, and to get some fresh air. I told my wife that I needed her to be there for a while so that I could have my own space to refresh myself.

I remembered there was an incident when my wife was not around, and I needed to leave the ward because I was feeling unwell. A churchmate happened to call me at that time and check with me if she could visit. I told her, "Please come," as I needed her to be there after her work because I was not feeling well. Thank God that she came to relieve my care for Ariel, and I was able to be away for a while. I felt much better after a short thirty minute break.

Another thing which we found difficult to talk about was asking for financial help. In Ariel's case, it was a prolonged medical condition that involved high medical expenses. Our family members and friends are definitely aware of our situation. Some gave automatically but some did not. Some even asked, "Do you need any financial help?"

I would say, "Yes. Do pray for us that God will provide for Ariel's medical needs." In this way, I didn't directly ask my friends to give but they were aware of our needs.

To tell you honestly, most of our friends were likely to respond to our requests, but they didn't quite know how to because we didn't tell them what we wanted specifically. They were also cautious about asking too many questions for fear of intruding into our privacy. That is where as a parent-in-need, I had to put aside my pride and say the three most important words, "I need you to buy me dinner. I need you to pray for our finances. I need you to fetch my wife here."

When we were able to say, "I need you", that was when we were able to find a lot of practical love and encouragement in the community.

2. Reach out to others in need

One of the most eye-opening experiences for me in my stay in the hospital was coming across patients with very challenging medical conditions.

I saw a three-year-old-girl, Yuan Yuan, who has been confined to her bed since birth. She has a congenital condition that required a kidney transplant. She could only go out of her ward for two hours during Chinese New Year every year. That was her life. As her parents needed to go to work, they engaged a maid to be with her full time. The only hope for her was to undergo a kidney transplant when she is about ten years old. That was the treatment plan for her. It was so depressing to hear that. When I talked to the maid and the nurses who attended to Yuan Yuan's needs, I felt that Ariel's condition was not so bad after all. At least, she still had Daddy and Mummy with her during her stay at the hospital.

I also met a seventeen-year-old boy, Jonathan, who had undergone a liver transplant when he was about three years old. In spite of frequent admissions to the hospital due to infections and viral attacks, he took things positively. He came to the hospital and saw his doctor all by himself. I had never seen his parents before. As I interacted with him, I got to know that he was behind his peers academically due to unpredictable virus attacks that disrupted his studies frequently. What amazed me most was his positive attitude. He took all these interruptions as part of his life and lived joyfully unto God moment by moment. He believed that Jesus had a wonderful plan for him—a living testimony of how one's religious faith could make a vast difference in one's outlook in life. Each time I saw him, I was inspired by him to trust Jesus more daily.

Another thing that really kept me going was serving the community around my church. I was in charge of my church's community outreach projects. I was tempted to quit when I first discovered Ariel's medical condition. "How can I take care of other people's needs when I am in need myself?" I reasoned to myself. As I prayed about my decision, God impressed upon my heart to continue to serve the community. Indeed, I was blessed by this decision. In my community, I saw many elderly in need. They were those who were handicapped, waiting for volunteers to bring them to the doctors or deliver their meals; those without any family members to take care of them; those with mentally-retarded children; those who were suffering from life-threatening diseases such as diabetes and strokes. In short, the outcasts of society.

My heart reached out to Yuan Yuan, Jonathan and those elderly in need. Their suffering helped me to forget my own suffering. Their resilience and calmness in the midst of their own suffering caused me to see hope in my own suffering. They were the living models of faith to me.

3. Insist on reaching a consensus between husband and wife
When a husband and wife stand together in the face of a crisis, they are like a mighty fortress. To reach a consensus between us, we spent a great amount of time communicating our thoughts, ideas and emotions to each other. Sometimes we agreed with one another, sometimes we didn't. At the end of the day, it was important to agree to disagree and commit any important decision to God in prayer. As a result, we became very close to each other as we shared tears and joys together.

The toughest decision was for my wife to consider being a living donor for Ariel. Though the fatality rate was only two percent, if that happened, it would have been one hundred percent for my wife. This was exactly what happened to my father who died during his heart bypass operation. It was a trauma that we never expected. The question we kept asking ourselves was, "If my wife turns out to be another patient, could we handle two young children and two critically ill patients? It would be a horrible nightmare for us." As I listened empathetically to my wife as she shared her fears and concerns, I could only nod in agreement. After all, it was her own liver. No one could imagine the aftermath of giving part of your organ away. Would it affect her health and lifestyle? Nobody knew for sure.

When my wife finally decided to be a living donor, I supported her decision, knowing full well the possible risks that might happen to our family. I also understood that as a mummy to Ariel, she could not stand the sight of seeing Ariel dying as each day passed when she could do something to help her.

I was not always a saint to my wife. There were moments that I lashed out in anger at her when I couldn't stand her irrational fears and emotions. In retrospect, I knew I shouldn't have, but it did happen. I couldn't pretend that nothing had happened. As a result, we entered into a 'Cold War'. I could still remember those times when I needed her reply with regard to Ariel's situation, but she didn't give one. I was mad at her. I felt that she had gone overboard with her emotions. So I called her best friend to intervene because I was at a loss as to how to handle my relationship with my wife. Thankfully we were able to resolve this difference and continue our challenging parenting journey.

To be honest, I have seen a husband walk out of his marriage because he couldn't handle a medically-challenging child. The intensity of such a stressor was very real. As husband and wife, we could either let this stressor draw us closer together or away from each other. Understanding, communication and the support of friends are essential elements to foster consensus between us as husband and wife.

4. Adopt a balanced approach

There were many alternative treatments for treating Ariel. When we were told by a Western doctor that all they could do was to prepare Ariel for a liver transplant, we were not in favour of that option. The reason was because even after Ariel goes through a liver transplant successfully, she has to be on lifelong anti-rejection medication and it can have side effects on her kidneys and other organs in the long run.

Therefore the first treatment that we had chosen was Traditional Chinese Medicine (TCM). We felt that since Western treatments couldn't help her condition, we would try Eastern treatments. We went around searching for the best TCM doctor who had experience in treating babies with liver problems, but the effort was in vain. The closest that we could find was a TCM doctor who had successfully treated adults with liver problems. He had never tried his techniques on a baby before because most parents would prefer sending their babies to see Western doctors than to him. We decided to give it a shot anyway. We tried it for a few months but found no visible improvement. We were discouraged.

The next thing we reasoned was that as Christians we would trust God for healing and nothing else as we sincerely believed that our God is able to heal. We brought Ariel for healing services at different churches and partook Holy

Communion to ask God to heal her. At the same time, we came across an alternative treatment called "Jin Shin Jyutsu", recommended by a Polytechnic lecturer when she came to the hospital to supervise her nursing students. She told us that Jin Shin Jyutsu might be able to help Ariel. It was a Japanese art of treatment based on the belief that our hands had the ability to heal by pressing on certain acupressure points on the body to harmonise the energy flow. We consulted Prof. Quak, the doctor in charge of Ariel about this form of treatment. As expected, he had no objection to it, as he saw no harm trying this on Ariel. We concurred with him and decided to go for it.

Making an appointment with Ms. Siew Kim, the founder of Jin Shin Jyutsu in Singapore, was a challenge. Her schedule was so packed that the only time we could see her was during her lunch time. Her treatment fee was one hundred dollars for a forty-minute session. But God was gracious to us. After seeing Ariel for the first time, Siew Kim had such compassion for Ariel that she decided to waive the treatment fee. She told us that since Ariel was a baby, she could only treat Ariel for fifteen minutes per session and she needed to see Ariel twice a week; and it would be free. We were touched by Siew Kim's kindness towards us. So we faithfully brought Ariel to see her twice a week without fail except during Ariel's admission. Siew Kim also taught us how to press her acupressure points, and we were supposed to do it every night before she slept.

Honestly speaking, we couldn't tell if Jin Shin Jyutsu did help Ariel. But it was something we could do for her whether she was at home or at the hospital.

When Ariel was about two-and-a-half years old, we were confronted by the hard fact that she needed a liver transplant as soon as possible. Prof. Quak hinted this to us when Ariel was about two years old, but we were not open to it. We told him that we believed that our God could heal her. Finally, he had to tell us bluntly that if we chose to ignore the liver transplant as an option, we might lose her forever. It was either "now" when she was healthy enough to receive a new liver or "never" when she becomes too sick for any major operation.

It was like a bomb exploding in our heads. We were suddenly awakened to the fact that we needed to take the possibility of a liver transplant seriously. As much as we wanted to trust God for His miraculous healing, we couldn't deny that medical intervention by a liver transplant could be His will for her, too. We knew that the chances of a liver transplant to take place was equivalent to striking the lottery because most patients die while waiting for their donors. We felt that we needed to maintain a fine balance between our Christian faith and human intervention. Finally, we decided to trust God to do whatever He knew was best for Ariel by putting her on the waiting list for a liver transplant.

We needed to ask God for wisdom to have a holistic and balanced approach towards treatment; between

Western and Eastern treatments, between conventional and alternative treatment, and between supernatural healing and medical technology.

5. Lay hold of God's promises

My constant source of strength and encouragement during this difficult three-year journey was my faith in and focus on my God and Saviour, Jesus Christ. Circumstances and people might fail us but God never does.

The attributes of God that carried me through this time is that He is strong and loving at the same time.

God assured me that He was strong and powerful enough to save Ariel since He was the Creator of all things. I remembered an incident when I went to a little garden outside the ward to pray. In my solitude, I saw some ants trying to build something on the ground. They worked very hard, trying to stack tiny little pieces of leaves on top of one another. I was curious, so I looked at them intently to ensure that everything was smooth-going for them.

Then it dawned upon me that my creator God was like that, too. I was a giant to these ants just like God was a giant to me. Just like I was powerful enough to intervene anytime with what the ants were doing, this was true for my God, too. I found comfort in knowing that He was mighty and near enough to intervene in Ariel's situation anytime He desired.

Not only that, my God was also overflowing with compassion. The Bible told me that He never desires seeing His children suffer. He is grieved to see His children in sorrow. It is never in His will and pleasure. However, sometimes He permits suffering to reveal His unknown purposes to His children. In short, God is love and suffering is not His desired will but His permissible will.

These two attributes of God—that He is powerful and loving—are important to me. If God is powerful, but not loving, He wouldn't care about my suffering. On the other hand, if God is loving but not powerful, what if He cares about my suffering but does not have the ability to change anything? When I knew that God cared for me and could intervene in my affairs anytime, I dared not give up. I would hold on to my faith and hope till Ariel's last breath.

I had initiated three cycles of prayer with fasting—a forty-day fast; a two-week fast and a twenty-one-day fast. These were moments of desperation and intercession for Ariel's life. Most importantly, I was drawn closer to God's heartbeat for Ariel and my family. On hindsight, I would never like to go through that again. However, those were my most intimate moments with Jesus—the milestones of my spiritual journey.

Laying hold of God's promises in my darkest moments is the most important thing I can do when everything seems bleak and hopeless. Without Jesus, I am nothing, and I can't do anything during a crisis that is beyond human control.

If you desire to know my God personally, I would like to encourage you to read more about Him in Appendix C— "The Best Decision I Have Ever Made in my Life".

THE BEST DECISION I'VE EVER MADE

*H*ave you heard of the Four Spiritual Laws?

Just as there are physical laws that govern them physical universe, so are there spiritual laws which govern your relationship with God.

LAW 1

God LOVES you and offers a wonderful PLAN for your life.

(References contained in this booklet should be read in context from the Bible whenever possible)

GOD'S LOVE

"God so loved the world that He gave His one and only Son, that whoever believes in Him shall not perish, but have eternal life" (John 3:16, NIV).

GOD'S PLAN

[Christ speaking] "I came that they might have life, and might have it abundantly" [that it might be full and meaningful] (John 10:10).

Why is it that most people are not experiencing the abundant life? Because...

LAW 2

Man is SINFUL and SEPARATED from God. Thus, he cannot know and experience God's love and plan for his life.

MAN IS SINFUL

"All have sinned and fall short of the glory of God" (Romans 3:23).

Man was created to have fellowship with God; but, because of his stubborn self-will, he chose to go his own independent way, and fellowship with God was broken. This self-will, characterised by an attitude of active rebellion or passive indifference, is an evidence of what the Bible calls sin.

MAN IS SEPARATED

"The wages of sin is death" [spiritual separation from God] (Romans 6:23).

This diagram illustrates that God is holy and man is sinful. A great gulf separates the two. The arrows illustrate that man is continually trying to reach God and the abundant life through his own efforts, such as a good life, philosophy, or religion—but he inevitably fails.

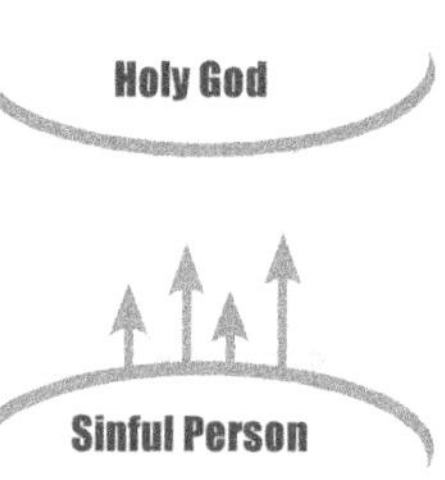

The third law explains the only way to bridge this gulf...

LAW 3

Jesus Christ is God's ONLY provision for man's sin. Through Him you can know and experience God's love and plan for your life.

HE DIED IN OUR PLACE

"God demonstrates His own love toward us, in that while we were yet sinners, Christ died for us" (Romans 5:8).

HE ROSE FROM THE DEAD

"Christ died for our sins...He was buried...He was raised on the third day, according to the Scriptures...He appeared to Peter, then to the twelve. After that He appeared to more than five hundred...." (1 Corinthians 15:3-6).

HE IS THE ONLY WAY TO GOD

"Jesus said to him, 'I am the way, and the truth, and the life; no one comes to the Father, but through Me'" (John 14:6).

This diagram illustrates that God has bridged the gulf which separates us from Him by sending His Son, Jesus Christ, to die on the cross in our place to pay the penalty for our sins.

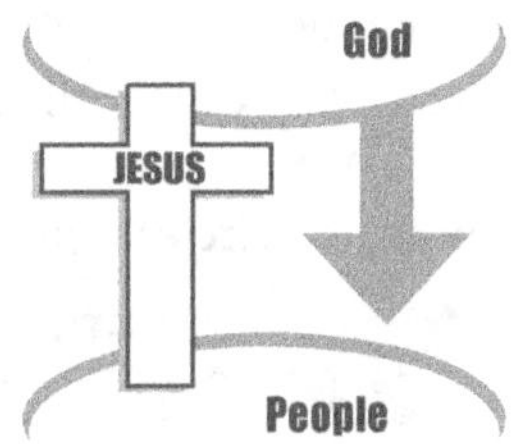

It is not enough just to know these three laws…

LAW 4

We must individually RECEIVE Jesus Christ as Saviour and Lord; then we can know and experience God's love and plan for our lives.

WE MUST RECEIVE CHRIST

"As many as received Him, to them He gave the right to become children of God, even to those who believe in His name" (John 1:12)

WE RECEIVE CHRIST THROUGH FAITH

"By grace you have been saved through faith; and that not of yourselves, it is the gift of God; not as a result of works, that no one should boast" (Ephesians 2:8-9).

WHEN WE RECEIVE CHRIST, WE EXPERIENCE A NEW BIRTH (Read John 3:1-8)

WE RECEIVE CHRIST BY PERSONAL INVITATION

[Christ speaking] "Behold, I stand at the door and knock; if any one hears My voice and opens the door, I will come in to him" (Revelation 3:20).

Receiving Christ involves turning to God from self (repentance) and trusting Christ to come into our lives to forgive our sins and to make us what He wants us to be. Just to agree **intellectually** that Jesus Christ is the Son of God and that He died on the cross for our sins is not enough. Nor is it enough to have an **emotional** experience. We receive Jesus Christ by **faith**, as an act of the **will**.

These two circles represent two kinds of lives:

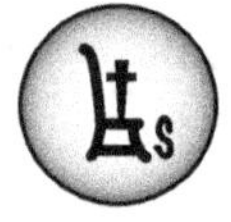

SELF-DIRECTED LIFE

S - Self is on the throne of the life   **†** - Jesus Christ is outside the life

Their interests are directed by self.
They do not know God and have not received forgiveness for their sins and remain cut off from God.

CHRIST-DIRECTED LIFE

† - Jesus Christ is on the throne of life
S - Self submits to Jesus for Him to direct

They have repented of their sins and received Christ into their lives. They experience God's love and forgiveness, and willingly obey Christ as Lord.

Which circle best describes your life?

Which circle would you like to have represent your life?

The following explains how you can receive Christ:

YOU CAN RECEIVE CHRIST RIGHT NOW BY FAITH THROUGH PRAYER (Prayer is talking to God)

God knows your heart and is not so concerned with your words as He is with the attitude of your heart. The following is a suggested prayer:

"Lord Jesus, I need You. Thank You for dying on the cross for my sins. I open the door of my life and receive You as my Saviour and Lord. Thank You for forgiving my sins and giving me eternal life. Take control of the throne of my life. Make me the kind of person You want me to be. Amen."

Does this prayer express the desire of your heart?

If it does, I invite you to pray this prayer right now, and Christ will come into your life, as He promised.

HOW TO KNOW THAT CHRIST IS IN YOUR LIFE

Did you receive Christ into your life? According to His promise in Revelation 3:20, where is Christ right now in relation to you? Christ said that He would come into your life. Would He mislead you? On what authority do you know that God has answered your prayer? (The trustworthiness of God Himself and His Word.)

THE BIBLE PROMISES ETERNAL LIFE

"The witness is this, that God has given us eternal life, and this life is in His Son. He who has the Son has the life; he who does not have the Son of God does not have life. These things I have written to you who believe in the name of the Son of God, in order that you may **know** that you have eternal life" (1 John 5:11-13).

Thank God often that Christ is in your life and that He will never leave you (Hebrews 13:5). You can know on the basis of His promise that Christ lives in you and that you have eternal life from the very moment you invite Him in. He will not deceive you.

An important reminder..

DO NOT DEPEND ON FEELINGS

The promise of God's Word, the Bible—not our feelings—is our authority. The Christian lives by faith (trust) in the trustworthiness of God Himself and His Word. This train diagram illustrates the relationship among **fact** (God and His Word), **faith** (our trust in God and His Word), and **feeling** (the result of our faith and obedience). (John 14:21)

The train will run with or without the passenger car. However, it would be useless to attempt to pull the train by the passenger car. In the same

way, as Christians we do not depend on feelings or emotions, but we place our faith (trust) in the trustworthiness of God and the promises of His Word.

NOW THAT YOU HAVE RECEIVED CHRIST

The moment that you received Christ by faith, as an act of the will, many things happened, including the following:

1. Christ came into your life through the Holy Spirit into your heart (Revelation 3:20; Colossians 1:27).

2. Your sins were forgiven (Colossians 1:14).

3. You became a child of God (John 1:12).

4. You received eternal life (John 5:24).

5. You began the great adventure for which God created you (John 10:10, 2 Corinthians 5:17, 1 Thessalonians 5:18).

Can you think of anything more wonderful that could happen to you than receiving Christ? Would you like to thank God in prayer right now for what He has done for you? By thanking God, you demonstrate your faith.

To enjoy your new life to the fullest...

SUGGESTIONS FOR CHRISTIAN GROWTH

Spiritual growth results from trusting Jesus Christ. "The righteous man shall live by faith" (Galatians 3:11). A life of faith will enable you to trust God increasingly with every detail of your life, and to practice the following:

G Go to God in prayer daily (John 15:7).

R Read God's Word daily (Acts 17:11); begin with the Gospel of John.

O Obey God moment by moment (John 14:21).

W Witness for Christ by your life and words (Matthew 4:19; John 15:8).

T Trust God for every detail of your life (1 Peter 5:7).

H Holy Spirit—allow Him to control and empower your daily life and witness (Galatians 5:16,17; Acts 1:8).

FELLOWSHIP IN A GOOD CHURCH

God's Word instructs us "not to forsake the assembling of ourselves together" (Hebrews 10:25). Several logs burn brightly together; but put one aside on the cold hearth and the fire goes out. So it is with your relationship with other Christians.

If you do not belong to a church, do not wait to be invited. Take the initiative; call or visit a nearby church where Christ is honoured and His Word is preached. Start this week, and make plans to attend regularly.

Special Materials Are Available for Christian Growth

If you have come to know Christ personally through this presentation of the gospel, helpful materials for Christian growth are available to you. For more information, write to: Cru Singapore, c/o Cru Asia Ltd, My SingPost Box 880052, Singapore 919191, Email: admin@cru.org.sg; Website: http://www.cru.org.sg

If you have made a decision to receive Jesus into your life, I would like to hear from you. Do email Moses at moses@journeywithu.com or leave your comment on my website: www.journeywithu.com

"I AM FOREVER GRATEFUL"

I am forever grateful to God for the miracle.

26 Dec 2008, Fri

I have just been discharged from the hospital from another life-threatening internal bleeding. I had lost count of the number of times I was hospitalised due to internal bleeding in the last six months. Physically emaciated and dying, I could not eat well and respond much to people around me. I remember I would gaze lifelessly at my family members engaging busily with their daily activities. I wished to join them but I was too weak to do so.

I saw my parents kneel several times before God, praying and weeping throughout the day. Then, Mummy approached me and asked, "Ariel, do you want to live?" I nodded. "If you want, then you must tell God yourself. Tell Him to give you a new life today."

Though it was a beautiful Saturday, I was too feeble and lethargic to enjoy it. I could not remember how long I was lying on my favourite mattress when the ringing of the phone interrupted my thoughts. It was from the National University Hospital. It brought God's miracle—a liver for me! How could it be? In the past few months, I have heard doctors and all relevant medical staff tell us that it was not likely I could get a liver. It was like waiting for a one in a million thing.

28 Dec 2008 till 28 Jan 2009

It was an extremely difficult month for me. I had absolutely no idea of the things happening after I was pushed into the operating theatre. The moment I came round, I was in great distress as there were eight big tubes piercing into my frail little body.

Thereafter, a series of complications occurred to me. One of the worst complications which threw all of us off was the constant influx of great amount of fluids into my belly. Every day, I was heavily laden with about three kilogrammes of fluids in my little tummy. It ballooned and became so big that I thought it would burst anytime. Doctors told my parents that I might have to carry it for six months. However, it was God's mercy that the fluids subsided within two months.

So far, I have been given an excellent prognosis for my post-transplant condition. Now, the scar etched across my tummy is a beautiful remembrance of God's miracle and mercy to my family and me.

I am forever grateful to God for the donor's family—their beloved child was pronounced brain dead suddenly. Feeling distraught and devastated, they could have chosen to keep all their child's organs intact and of course, they had the right to do so. Despite their emotional and mental anguish, they made a noble decision after a few days of consideration. They decided to donate all the healthy organs and I was one of the blessed ones who received the timely gift. How could I be more grateful than this—someone had to lose his precious gift of life in order to give me life.

Through it, I have a deeper appreciation of God's ineffable love for me. He had to lose His only begotten child, Jesus for me so that I can live eternally.

I am forever grateful to God for healing me.

2 to 6 August 2009

I contracted the H1N1 virus from my brother. My parents were worried if I could get well as I was on a high dosage of anti-rejection medication. It suppresses my natural anti-bodies that could fight against any foreign viruses. So, it was highly possible that the H1N1 virus could overcome me easily at any point in time.

Besides, I was not the only one coming down with the virus. My whole family except Daddy was in the throes of sickness. God is good, we were as right as rain within a week.

And I am forever grateful to God for all of you.

During my first three years of life, you had been supporting us faithfully in prayer and in many heart-warming ways. I know well that it would be difficult for my family to walk the arduous road of faith without your support. Your tangible help expressed God's love so evidently that we saw Jesus constantly throughout our ordeal.

My heartfelt thanks to all of you.

And I am forever grateful

Ariel Wong
Third daughter of Moses and Charissa
(The above is written by Charissa Wong)

ACKNOWLEDGEMENTS

First and foremost, I would like to give glory to my God, Jesus Christ who provides all the resources needed to make this book possible.

It is my special privilege to write about Jesus' story in my family life especially His miraculous work in Ariel's life. This story is about God's calling and mission in my life; to bring His message of hope and love for parents with medically-challenging children. I would like to encourage parents with this message; as parents we will never, never give up on our children. Tough times don't last, but tough people do.

Special thanks go to Gideon, who helped to craft my story in such a way that is compelling for the readers; and Elise from Cru Singapore for co-ordinating the editorial, internal layout and printing of my book.

There are too many people that I could thank God for. To list them down one by one will take eternity.

However, I would like to mention few key people who have made a significant impact in our lives; Rev. Lim Pang Jong of Toong Chai Presbyterian Church, Mr. Chua Siang Guan of St. Hilda Church, Rev. Lam Kok Hiang of Cru Singapore. Thank you for initiating to raise funds for Ariel's medical needs.

Thank God also for Prof. Quak Seng Hock and Prof. Praba from National University Hospital. Thank you for your professionalism and medical care for Ariel.

Thank God for Ms. Lim Siew Kim, founder of Jin Shin Juyutsu in Singapore, for assuring us constantly that Ariel would be fine under your treatment.

Last but not the least, I would like to thank God for my best friend and partner-in-life, Charissa for her unwavering faith in my leadership at home. Thank God also for my four awesome kids whom I fondly call them ACES; Ariel, Chloe, Ezekiel and Shiloh. Thank you teaching me to be a better Daddy. I love all of you!

BOOK SPONSORS

I would like to give a special acknowledgement to these book sponsors, who believe in my message and make the publishing of this book a reality. They are:

1. Liew Ying Hock
2. Derrick
3. Angelina
4. Ee Boon Ai
5. Denise Cheng
6. Tang Jui Guan
7. Andrew & Gace
8. Goh Keng Hock
9. Low Kum Seng
10. Hazel Tan
11. Clement Cheong
12. KhooWee Chuan
13. Stella Siak
14. Leong Sing Meng
15. Alan & Chia Min
16. Teoh Song Teng
17. Vincent Mak
18. Jason Wong
19. Khoo Lay Kuan
20. Elaine and Lawrence
21. Pastor Alvin Toh
22. Wah Chee & Yenny
23. Yap Chee Ping Anthony
24. Kok Hoong & Natalie

25. Dr Loh York King
26. Cheryl Fan
27. Chor Swee Sin
28. Dr Benjamin Cheah
29. Lim Kia Huan
30. Dickie Tan Swee Keong
31. Mina Wong
32. Ng Shi Cheng David
33. Tay Choon Mong
34. Rachel Tey
35. Ng Hwee Hong
36. Tay Yong Thai
37. Tan Kim Lian
38. Eileen Magnus
39. Alice Tan
40. Goh Chin Chin
41. Liew Zhi Wei
42. Derrick Goh
43. Aileen Tan
44. Pastor Yu Li Hsin Lisa
45. Ronald Lim
46. Phyllis Kew
47. Claire Tay
48. Chiang Teik Weng
49. John Eng
50. Judy Koh
51. Esther Lee
52. Dawn Liong
53. Ronald & Faye
54. Liu Yu Qing

Thank you for being my great supporter. I am eternally grateful for all of you. As promised, where my book goes, your name will be as well.

SPECIAL BONUS
FROM MOSES WONG

Now that you have your copy of *"From Trial to Triumph"*, you are on your way to creating effective strategies for coping with your child that has medical challenges. Plus, you will be inspired with the hope and love to continue your journey with your kids.

You'll also receive the special bonus I have created to add to your toolkit—"Five Helpful Principles in Overcoming Trials", which is a list of pointers that helped me to move from trial to triumph. These will serve as great reminders to help you sustain your faith and hope on this journey. Post this page in a place where you can review it daily.

There's so much confusing information out there about how to stay grounded in your faith when you are faced with significant challenges with your kids. When you finish this book, you'll be armed with what you need to know to not only cope with the situation but to strengthen your faith and trust in God's grace and unending love.

While "Five Helpful Principles in Overcoming Trials" is offered for sale, as a special gift from me, you can claim it for free here: http://FromTrialtoTriumphBook.com/gift

The sooner you discover and apply effective ways to cope with the medical situation of your child, the sooner you can help your family and grow spiritually from what may appear to be a very dire situation.

May the messages in this book help you find hope, inspiration, and love to continue the journey with grace and gratitude.

Moses

ABOUT THE AUTHOR

Moses graduated with a second class honours degree in Civil Engineering from the National University of Singapore in 1994. However, instead of practicing as an engineer, he went to serve in a not-for-profit organisation called Singapore Campus Crusade for Christ (now known as Cru Singapore) because of his passion to create a positive influence among the youth.

Throughout his sixteen years with SCCC (1994 to 2010), he served in several capacities such as team leader, prayer co-ordinator for four polytechnics and HR Manager, overseeing staff development.

Because of his great love for God and His people, he pursued a double Masters, a Masters of Arts in Pastoral Counselling and a Masters of Divinity with East Asia School of Theology, where he was awarded the Best Academic Award.

Currently, he is Managing Director of Journey With U Pte Ltd, an organisation that is dedicated to journeying with parents with challenged kids. This organisation is birthed by his deep desire to share the message of hope and love with parents after he has gone through three years of 'hell' with his third daughter, Ariel who was suffering from a terminal liver disease then.

Being a much sought-after family life educator whose programmes are pre-approved by the Ministry of Social and Family Development for funding, he has spoken to more than thousands of parents at different schools throughout Singapore.

He can be contacted at moses@journeywithu.com

Notes

NOTES

 NOTES

More from the Author

http://journeywithu.com

www.facebook.com/journeywithyou

Share Your Thoughts

You can write to the author to
share your thoughts or feedback at
moses@journeywithu.com or
http://journeywithu.com/bookblog

Be Empowered

Newsletter
Subscribe to our fortnightly newsletter
that will empower you as parents.
http://journeywithu.com/#contact-us

*Workshop**
Sign up for a one-day life-changing,
practical workshop to learn how to manage your
challenged kids successfully.

Workshop covers:
1. How to grief successfully
2. How to overcome fear and death victoriously
3. How to manage negative emotions positively
4. How to come up with practical strategies to deal with
your current situation

** In appreciation of your support to us, a special discount will be
given to you when you sign up for any of our courses.
Check our website for more information.*

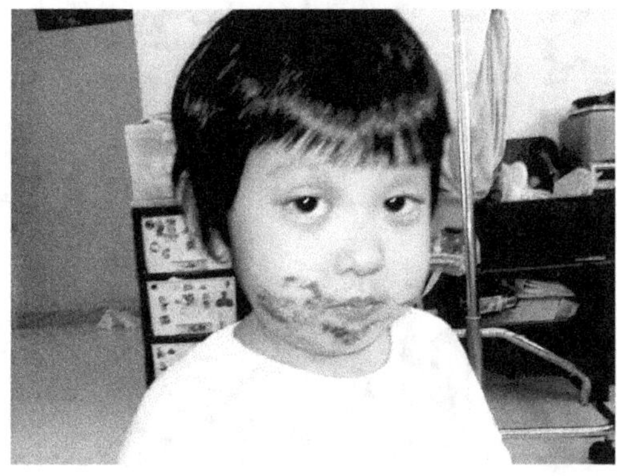

She is a normal child too.
She likes chocolate.

A birthday celebration with
my mum. We tried not to
restrict ourselves and lived our
lives as normally as we could.

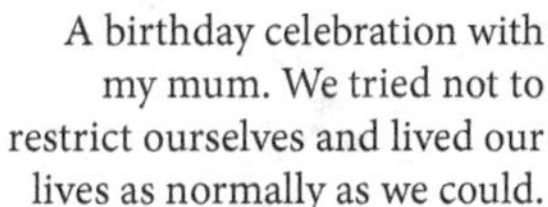

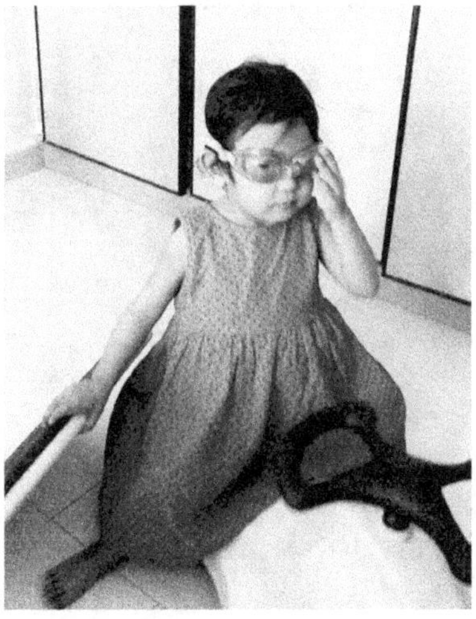

Though she could not stand well
because of her bloated tummy and
scrawny legs, she still played around
the house using her own vehicle.

Making her happy
whenever we could!

Her medical record for 2008 alone

Our attempts at giving her
a happy childhood

The cheeky side of Ariel

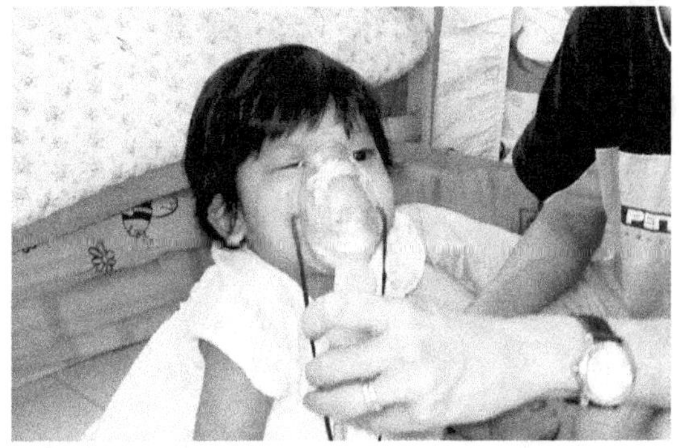

Whenever she has phlegm, we need to nebulise her. Thankful that the machine is sponsored by a church member.

My seven-year-old boy was a good helper too!

Ariel at her favourite place, the playground outside her ward

We are thankful that a group
of volunteers came and
celebrated Christmas with us.

Her last kiss to me
before they sedated her
for the transplant

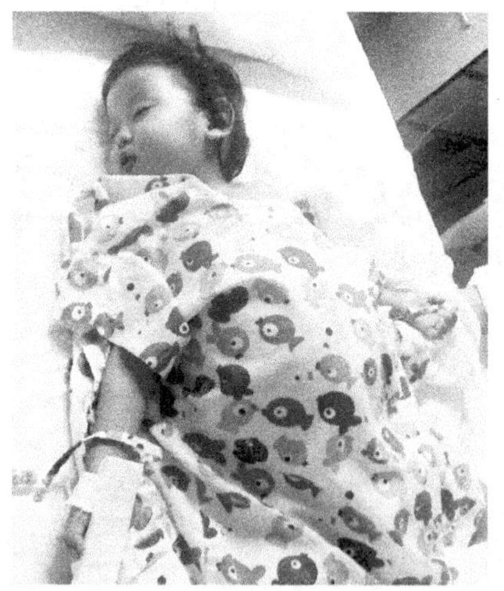

A few hours before the
transplant operation
was to take place

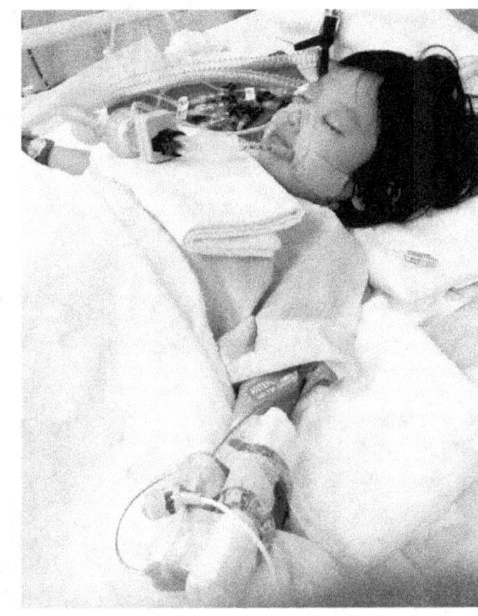

Immediately after the transplant,
my heart was broken

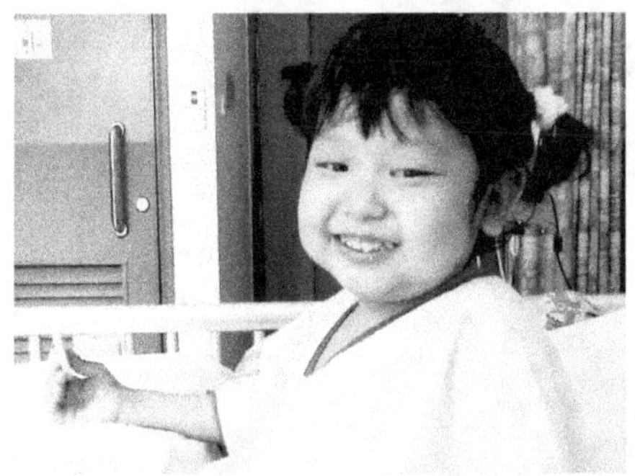

The side effects of the anti-
suppressant medication,
which made her cheeks puff up

Three months
after her transplant,
when she was three

Her fifth birthday

Her first day in
kindergarten

Family photo
taken during the
Lunar New Year.
Ariel was nine.